FOR THE LOVE
OF LETTERS

FOR THE LOVE OF LETTERS

A 21st-Century Guide to the Art of
Letter Writing

SAMARA O'SHEA

Collins
An Imprint of HarperCollinsPublishers

This book is dedicated to the graduate: Kathryn Taylor Stroup, MD.
My inspiration. My support. My cousin. My friend.
My first and ever-faithful pen pal.

Grateful acknowledgement is made for permission to quote from the following materials:

The Divine Sarah: A Life of Sarah Bernhardt by Arthur Gold and Robert Fizdale, copyright © 1991 by Robert Fizdale. Used by permission of Alfred A. Knopf, a division of Random House, Inc.

Letter Writing Guide for Amnesty International USA and the Urgent Action Network by AI-USA Urgent Action Program, copyright July 2005 by Amnesty International USA. Used by permission of Amnesty International USA.

"Talking Back: Letters from Readers" *Vogue*, November 2005.

"Letters from France and England" *Vogue*, July 15, 1940.

© Copyright 1940, 2005 Condé Nast Publications. All rights reserved. Originally published in *Vogue*. Reprinted with permission.

HarperCollins books may be purchased for educational, business, or sales promotional use. For information please write: Special Markets Department, HarperCollins Publishers, 10 East 53rd Street, New York, NY 10022.

FIRST EDITION

Designed by Paula Russell Szafranski

Library of Congress Cataloging-in-Publication Data

O'Shea, Samara.
   For the love of letters : a 21st-century guide to the art of letter writing. / Samara O'Shea.
—1st ed.
     p. cm
   ISBN: 978-0-06-121530-8
   ISBN-10: 0-06-121530-9
    1. Letter writing.   2. English language—Rhetoric.   I. Title.

PE1483.O83 2007
808.6—dc22

2006051813

07 08 09 10 WBC/FF 10 9 8 7 6 5 4 3 2 1

TABLE OF CONTENTS

Contents

CHAPTER SEVEN: *If We Must, We Must*

Yes, There's Still a Need for Letters

The art of general letter-writing in the present day is shrinking until
the letter threatens to become a telegram, a telephone message, a
post-card.

—EMILY POST, *ETIQUETTE*, 1922

"Do you know what ROFL stands for?" my mother asks. I can hear
in her voice that she already knows the answer and is ready to boast
about it.

"Rolling on the floor laughing!" Her animated reply practically
sends her into the act she just described.

"How about LOL?"

"No."

"Laugh out loud!"

I felt silly for not knowing that one. "Well, if I had seen it written I
would have known."

She continued, "TTYL? Talk to you later. JK? Just kidding. GTG?
Got to go."

My mother is mastering this new language à la acronyms so she can
communicate with my cousin Kimi. Thirteen-year-old Kimi is a quick
draw—the fastest text messager east of the Hudson River. I imagine
Kimi trapped at a family event without her cell phone, unable to

thumb-tap her way into the latest gossip circling among her friends—a tragic sight. I could tell her it won't always be like that, but she'd never believe me. I could also tell her there once was a time when thirteen-year-old me had to endure family gatherings without instant access to my friends. Occasionally I could sneak off and use the phone, but it wouldn't take long before the "Samara, where are you?" horn started to sound. Kimi knows nothing of this. She can sit quietly in the room, seemingly with us, but really she's at a friend's house or the mall—talking about newly formed crushes and horrid homework assignments.

It didn't take long for my mother to savvy up and accept if she was going to get to know the newly minted teenage version of her niece, she would have to do it on Kimi's terms—via computer or handheld gadget. Truthfully, I don't know what I find more amusing: Kimi's incessant IMing and texting or my mother's foray into the new experience. She confesses, "It took me forever to get BRB (be right back) and BBL (be back later). Kimi uses these a lot, and I'd be stranded typing, 'Kimi, what are you doing? Kimi, where are you? Kimi, why are you coming and going so much?'"

It may seem as though I've set this up to criticize the tenacity of technology and "kids today," but that's not the case. I completely understand and appreciate the need for shorthand and speed. If Friar Lawrence had had e-mail, Romeo and Juliet might have lived happily ever after. If Philippides had had his cell phone on him, he could have called in the good news of the Athenian army defeating the Persians instead of running twenty-some miles back to Athens only to die of exhaustion when he arrived.

My concern is, though, that what we gain in speed we lose in language—and, just a reminder, we are the heirs of a resplendent language. English is curvaceous, complex, and beautiful. Fluent and fierce. She is the lover you will always adore but will never fully know because there's too much to know. She is a true seductress—devious and overt, offering endless possibilities. With her I could tell you that you look gorgeous or that you look exquisite or that my body lost its breath when I happened upon you. When we encounter her placed in uncommon and alluring order we find inspiration and purpose. We find connection with ideas, with emotions, with people we know, with people we will never know, and with time periods that we must learn from and understand.

So I say yes, let's be efficient—but let's not squander our inheritance. Let the technology soar and improve, but let's be careful not to assume the latest and greatest inventions will be around forever. They most likely will not. Let's set time aside and allow our lovely language to bask in a place that has already proven its staying power: on paper. We must spread her out so that she can dazzle and breathe. Like all living things, if she does not breathe she will die.

How then do we keep her alive and healthy? We go back to the beginning. Before BlackBerries, text messages, instant messages, cell phones, fax machines, computers, typewriters, telephones, and telegraphs. We go back to a time when there were two things: language and paper. For writers, that combination equaled novels and articles. For the lovelorn, it equaled poetry. For mathematicians and scientists, it was a place to work out equations and take copious notes. For monks, it was a place to copy scripture. But for all these types, as well as the man on the street and the woman by the window, the person who just had a message to send, language plus paper equaled letters. And letters eventually equaled evidence. Evidence that they existed. That they breathed. That they had good insights and bad days. That they loved. That they suffered. That they longed. That they had moments of certifiable insanity. That they were selfish. And that, sometimes, they were satisfied. We must make arrangements for our descendants to discover us in such a candid way.

What brought us closer to the Holocaust but the diary and letters of a headstrong teenager who was forced to experience the changes of her body, frequent fights with her father, and the confusion of first love all in the confines of a stuffy attic? I remember reading years ago that one clever journalist had named Anne Frank Hitler's greatest enemy. What is the New Testament of *The Bible* really, but the selected letters of a few passionate young men excited to spread the message of their newfound faith? What woman doesn't swoon at the idea alone of a love letter written by Casanova or Valentino? And what person wouldn't find fascinating new insights into their favorite writer, philosopher, or politician when reading a collection of their letters?

On a recent trip to Nashville, I visited a historic home called the Belle Meade Plantation. Originally built in 1853, the astonishing home is filled with antiques and an acute sense of lives lived long ago. We were told that the house was restored to its original paint colors because they had found letters written by the mistress of the home delineating her plans to decorate. The mistress also wrote about the daily goings-on in her daughter's life, which at one point involved entertaining twenty-two young gentlemen suitors who came to call (at the same time!). We might not find our everyday lives too fascinating but our great-grandchildren will, and I'd much rather have them unfold a dusty sample of my enduring words than Google me.

Now, it's understandable if your children's children's children aren't the first thing on your mind in the morning—so don't write letters for them (just make sure you leave letters for them to find). Write letters for the people who are on your mind. Who are always on your mind. For the new love and the old friend. Thank the coworker who went out of her way to help you get adjusted. Empathize with your neighbor who just lost her son. Appease your wife after an unnecessary fight. Tell your husband about all the ways he still turns you on. Letters give messages backbone. They deliver what's written and they silently confess, "To me, you are worth the inconvenience of writing this letter."

Letters not only solidify history and fortify everyday events but they enact political change. Amnesty International (amnestyusa. org) has used letters to plead on behalf of human rights for more than 40 years, which is especially important in countries where Internet access is not readily available. The Global Aids Alliance website (globalaidsalliance.org) also asks its visitors to write letters to local government officials and heads of state. They offer e-mail as an option but suggest that printed letters send a stronger message. They provide form letters but also implore, "Please write your own letter—your words are more powerful than a form letter!"

And that is what I'd like you to take away from this book—an appreciation for how powerful your words are. How powerful our language is and how effective the two can be in tangible form. Letters instigate understanding, change, and closure. Letters are a chance for all of us to live well beyond our allotted years. They can and will affect the recipient, but what's oftentimes greater (and more surprising) is the effect letters have on the writer—who may be coming face-to-face with his or her thoughts and feelings for the first time. Letters have been performing acts—both ordinary and extraordinary—for several hundred millennia and I'd like to make sure they continue to do so.

I'll admit my fear of losing letters may be unfounded. As you saw above, Emily Post had the same fear in 1922 and letters are still with us, to a certain extent anyway. Just to be on the safe side, though, I'll sit Kimi down and explain everything to her, and she can explain what the heck BICBW* means.

*Because I could be wrong

Letter Writing and the Internet

What printing presses yield we think good store.
But what is writ by hand we reverence more.

—JOHN DONNE

I was born just in time. It was late 1970s and one electronic era was passing the torch to another. I have memories of my father's eight-track player, and I sang along to *Sesame Street* albums (I'm talking records here). I remember answering the phone before caller ID. I know what a busy signal sounds like. I know what the Dewey Decimal System is. And I recall life when computers were around—we had an Apple Tandy—but they were certainly not the necessity they are now. I was born just before the window shut; letters had a chance to play a purposeful role in my life before technology really persisted and threatened to eliminate them for good.

Let's fast-forward now twenty-five years past my dad's eight tracks. I'm in a café with my laptop. I'm between jobs and very antsy. Most of my energy goes into figuring out what I'm going to do next, and any creative juice I had left is channeled into my half-finished novel, a source of never-ending frustration. The unofficial rule is about to kick in—when a writer is restless, which is most of the time, the crazy ideas come.

My crazy idea was the sum of recent events and of me trying to create an occupation for myself. I asked: *If I could do anything, what would it be?* I answered: *I would sit in my castle in the clouds and write letters. People would come to me from far and wide with their tales of love and loss and I would help them find the words they were looking for.* The recent event that inspired this was my roommate had asked me to help her write a letter to a guy she was dating, and she was very happy with what I came up with. Now all I had to do was walk off my cloud and make it practical, so in true 21st-century form I turned immediately and ironically to the Internet to save the art of letter writing.

When I was ready to launch the Web site LetterLover.net—the letter-writing service of my dreams minus the castle and the clouds—in April 2005, reactions were mixed. Some friends smiled politely out of kindness, others didn't try to hide their bewilderment: "Huh?" I was outside with my laptop in Bryant Park and a man asked me what I was working on. I told him and he said, "That's actually brilliant." I think he was just trying to sleep with me. I ended up telling a friend of a friend at happy hour, and she caught me completely off guard by squealing with delight and congratulating me on having such an original idea. I was grateful for her enthusiasm but didn't have the heart to tell her that writing letters for other people is far from original—the concept is as old as letter writing itself.

Throughout history every culture and civilization has employed the art of scribes and letter writers, as the majority of the population did not receive a formal education and could not read or write. This practice worked its way well into the twentieth century. A friend of mine who lived in Izmir, Turkey, in the mid 1970s has vivid recollections of the letter writers who sat outside the post office and transcribed the lives of the illiterate. A day in the life of a letter writer is illustrated perfectly in the beginning of the movie *Central Station*—Golden Globe winner for best foreign language film in 1998. Dora, a retired schoolteacher, works as a letter writer for some of the 300,000 people who pass through Rio de Janeiro's main train station each day. The movie opens as her customers confess their lives. One woman is in tears as she dictates a letter to her lover who is in jail. An older man wants to write to someone who betrayed him and thank him for it while he wears an unmistakable expression of forgiveness on his face. An eager young man waxes poetic about his girlfriend's hot body and what he wants to do to it. Meanwhile, the letter writer stays stoic and writes what they ask, refusing to involve herself emotionally in their lives even though their emotions are all over the table. In the DVD's director's commentary it is noted that some of the people in the station asked if they could be a part of the film and dictate their real letters. Director Walter Salles permitted this and says that it ended up altering the texture of the story and bringing a reality to it.

Not all letter writers are out to help the illiterate; some are out to help the inarticulate. Playwright Edmond Rostand's most popular play, *Cyrano de Bergerac* (1897), tells the story of Cyrano—a man with an exceptionally large nose—who decides he'll never win the heart of his beloved, Roxane, because of his looks. He ends up helping the handsome but tongue-tied Christian pursue Roxane by writing letters to her on his behalf. This story experienced a 1980s-style revival in the movie *Roxanne* (1987), starring Steve Martin and Daryl Hannah. Here, Cyrano is renamed C.D. and Christian is simply called Chris. In the end Roxanne realizes it was C.D.'s sweet language she fell in love with rather than Chris's good looks.

For those of you who remember the short-lived yet significant series *My So-Called Life*, the show's finale had a similar plot. Irresistible Jordan Catalano employs the troubled but brilliant Brian Krakow to write a letter for ingénue Angela Chase. Jordan, needing to apologize and not knowing how, laments out loud, "It's gotta be written down so I can't screw it up." Brian says no at first but does end up writing the letter, as it's his only outlet to express his true feelings for Angela. In the end this story leans more toward real life than *Roxanne*. Angela knows Brian wrote the letter. She goes to Jordan anyway.

In *Roxanne*, when Chris first asks C.D. to write letters for him C.D. replies, "That's lying." And Chris says, "Not if you write what I feel." That's how I justified writing letters for people on my website—they gave me the ingredients, and I made the cake. What surprised me the most was that no one said, "Lady, are you for real?" They e-mailed me and launched right into their stories. I'm not exactly sure what made me feel qualified to do this. It was partly because I was a professional writer but more so because the range of human emotional experience is not that vast—we can all identify with each other to a certain degree. I knew I could draw inspiration from my own emotional history to articulate their lives. And that's how it went, they gave me stories, I gave them words, and it was up to them to deliver the message. Some probably copied it into their own hand, while others left them typed, and others e-mailed. Now is probably a good time to tell you that this is not an anti e-mail book. I'm a fan myself and have received many a moving letter via e-mail. For all the arbitrary e-mails that go back and forth, the passionate, meaningful, sometimes even hurtful ones make their way in there. Print these out. I mean it; these are your letters. Print them and put them in a shoebox. I have a friend who told me she stopped writing in her journal altogether because printing her e-mails told tales well enough. I leave room for e-mail in many cases throughout this book, but do suggest that print letters trump e-mail in certain situations and (believe it or not) vice versa.

Among those who adamantly disagreed with my business venture were two students from my alma mater, Duquesne University. There's guaranteed amusement in the student newspaper doing a story on you. "I don't understand why you wouldn't just do it yourself," said junior forensic science major Sara Huber. "I mean grow some balls and write a letter." Junior sociology major Becky Wilker agrees. She finds the whole Web site to be quite odd. "It's pretty ridiculous," Wilker said, "A letter is supposed to be personal."

In defense of my customers, I'm certain no one was writing me because they lacked metaphorical balls (the women obviously lacked physical balls). Some were just out of practice and others were never in practice. One woman wrote to me and started with "I am a terrible writer . . . I am an Equity Trader. Numbers r my thing writing no." Also, the site was launched to promote letter writing itself as much as me as the letter writer. If someone who hadn't been thinking of writing a letter saw my site and thought, "I can do this myself. I don't need her." Then I genuinely say, "Mission accomplished!"

Now, I'm never above admitting I might be wrong, so to my collegiate critics I say, "Ladies, perhaps you are correct and writing letters for other people is absolutely absurd. In which case, my time is best spent here with this book where I can tell you all that I've learned."

1   Letters as Gifts

Treasure these few words till we're together.
Keep all my love forever.
P.S. I Love You
—LENNON & MCCARTNEY

We are taught as children that the best gifts are homemade—that's a lesson we should never unlearn. What comes with a handmade gift is not only the gift itself but, more important, the invaluable time the other person put into it. All relationships need positive reinforcement on a regular basis, and priceless gifts are much more effective in accomplishing this than expensive ones. Letters fit the priceless bill perfectly not only because of the time but also the raw emotion and thought they require. If we take it to an extreme, I can say with certainty that a relationship where nothing but diamond bracelets and gold watches are exchanged would pale in comparison to a relationship where nothing but letters and roses stolen from the neighbor's yard are exchanged. Not that you shouldn't be grateful for a diamond bracelet—you know what I mean.

This isn't true of just romantic relationships either. Since the people who love us the most—mom, dad, sister Sue, and aunt Veronica—tend to be the people we take for granted the most, it never hurts to send an unexpected reminder that you think the world of them. It will be more cherished than the NASCAR tie you bought your father for his birthday. I promise.

LOVE LETTERS

I am pleased to announce that of all the letter requests I've received on my Web site, love letters are the highest in demand. I expected apology letters to be number one or even breakup letters, but no, love letters conquer all. Admittedly, I was surprised yet ecstatic because it made me feel that all is well with the universe. There are plenty of people walking around in love and looking for new ways of saying old things.

When I first launched LetterLover.net I received an immediate outpouring of support from my family and friends. Though I think most of them thought, *What is she doing?* The first two considerate acknowledgements came from my cousin Jennifer and her husband, Graham. Thoughtful gestures come naturally to these two and they both touched base with me unaware that the other was doing so. Jennifer sent my Web link to her friends and colleagues and gave me their feedback. Meanwhile, Graham took on the much-appreciated responsibility of being my first customer by requesting an eighth-anniversary letter for his lovely wife.

Practicing on people I know was an ideal way for me to get my feet wet. It also helped that Jennifer is an easy person to write a love letter for, since she gives people no choice but to admire her. She attended Boston College with the intention of being an English teacher but changed her mind and made getting an MBA from Harvard Business School appear effortless. She then went on to be a full-force woman in Manhattan's old-boys-club financial world and somehow found time to bear three children (all boys!). On top of this she happens to be a knockout—a blue-eyed, wide smile, she-couldn't-possibly-have-three-children knockout. Upon receipt, Jennifer obviously knew I wrote the following letter. But she also knew that Graham wouldn't dispute any of it and appreciated, no doubt, his motion of support toward me.

The Love Letter

Dear Jennifer,

We went into this eight years ago knowing to expect the un-expected, and we certainly haven't been disappointed. As far as life's surprises go, I'm still amazed at the way you balance our marriage, your career, and loving our boys with beauty and grace. You've accomplished so much since we first met, and I'm so proud to have participated in your three greatest accomplishments with you. I'm even prouder to know that our sons are being raised by a bright, ambitious, and faithful woman who continues to set exceptional examples for them— mothering three kings is no small task.

On a more selfish note, being seen with a slender, beau-tiful woman on my arm never EVER gets old. Thank you for embodying all things wonderful, and thank you for tak-ing such good care of me. In other words, I love you. And, believe it or not, I love you more than I did when we first got married.

There's still so much left for us to do, but I thought you might like to know (or be reminded anyway) that I'm your biggest fan. Thank you for taking this journey with me. Happy Anniversary.

Your-not-so-secret admirer, husband, and friend, Graham

Be Specific

Imagine, if you will, a room—a gathering—of all your old flames. I mean all of them—Gina from the fourth grade, Chris the sophomore soccer player, and hot, handsome Joe from last night. Now, let the sheer terror of this situation roll off your back—it's just a daydream.

Let's say that at some point you wrote love letters to all of them, and they are now going to stand in a circle and, one by one, read your letters aloud. My question is: Do your letters all say the same thing? Do you jump from relationship to relationship carrying with you the same compliments, same romantic turns of phrase, the same run-of-the-mill repertoire?

If you do, then don't. You've got a new and exciting person in front of you and they deserve new and exciting tokens of appreciation as unique as they are. Grant each person a version of your love that no one else will ever have access to. Even though things won't always work out, each relationship is significant and special in its own right and should be treated as such. Let this be reflected in your letters. So that if you ever did end up in the scary circle scenario it wouldn't be as awkward. With every letter read it would be clear that you noted and highlighted everyone's individual eccentricities. It would flatter them all to know they possess affections from you that no one else has ever or will ever receive.

I'll be the first to proclaim that there is no formula for love letters. Close your eyes and feel is the best advice I can give, but if you need help kick-starting the process, here are a few suggestions:

> *How to Start*   The first sentence of just about any written work is always the hardest. It is, however, slightly easier with love letters because there's no introduction required—you can get right to the point. One quick sentence and you're good to go. Try starting with a sense of urgency, "There's something very important that I need to tell you." Confessing a state of helplessness—both mentally and physically—also works well, "I'm sitting here unable to focus and barely able to breathe, as thoughts of you are taking on a life of their own."

> *Bring on the Adjectives*   Make a list of all the things you adore about the other person. For example: Bright, thoughtful,

driven, daring, beautiful, breathtaking, I-can't-stop-looking-at-you! You get the idea. Then use this list to craft the letter. Wrap a few sentences around each word. Like so: (Adjective = striking) "You know I didn't hear a word Chuck said when we were at his party because you were in that baby blue dress and everywhere I turned I could see you out of the corner of my eye. My God, you're a striking woman."

🖎 *Disguise Your Letter*   Camouflaging love letters as thank-you letters always gets a good response. Thank them for the things they do, "Thank you for washing my car last weekend." But also thank them for things they have little to no control over: "Thank you for making every day a truly unique experience—you are an unending mystery." Or "Thank you for looking so radiant when you first wake up. The sight of you is the perfect start to all my days."

🖎 *Ask Questions*   I find that clever, rhetorical questions work well as a flattering technique: Could you be any sexier? Could I look any better being seen with you? Could you be any sweeter? How could I possibly stop myself from falling for you?

🖎 *Take Note of the Time*   Pointing out the length of a relationship is an effective tool. If you've been together for a short time, write "I can't believe my feelings have grown so strong in only four months." If you've been together forever, then that certainly deserves a nod: "Well, would you look at that? After thirty years I think it's safe to say we beat the odds."

🖎 *Fake 'Em Out*   Please, forgive the reference I'm about to make: There's a Michael Bolton song, "Said I Loved You . . .

But I Lied," which sounds harsh, but the lyrics continue, "Said I loved you, but I lied. 'Cause this is more than love I feel inside." This misleading concept translates well to letters. You could write something like, "You, for some reason, find it necessary to distract me from work and from volleyball on a regular basis. Thank you so much for doing that."

Counteract the Clichés There are common compliments that we all need to hear—pretty eyes, lips, hair, naturally good-looking, talented, smart, funny, etc. Of course use these, but try to use them in a fresh way. Play with the words—it's fun. Well, I think it's fun. Instead of writing "You have beautiful eyes," try "I'm helpless in the presence of your electric eyes." Instead of "I love your smile," try something like "Your smile is my favorite distraction."

For Better or for Worse Every relationship has its sore spots. Some spots are huge issues and others are minor irritations that you eventually learn to laugh about. I suggest using the latter in your love letters. Let them know you love them with all their imperfections attached. For example: "You are still my favorite person, despite the pile of trash that always seems to be at my feet when I ride shotgun."

Role Reversal Think of a few compliments that your love may not be used to hearing because of their sex. You can tell a woman you admire her for her strength, courage, determination, and bulging biceps (okay, maybe not that last one). And I'm a firm believer that every man deserves to be told at least once in his life how beautiful he is, especially by the one who loves him.

Have fun You're not in trouble. They're not in trouble. There is no trouble. There is only satisfaction and delight.

If you find yourself sitting down to write a love letter, congratulations! You're in love, and that is a good place to be*.

Signing Off

- ✉ **Yours through time and eternity,** Civil War General George Armstrong Custer (1839–1876) ended a love letter to his wife, Elizabeth, this way.
- ✉ **Always, with undying love, yours,** An affectionate ending from Irish poet Oscar Wilde (1854–1900) to Lord Alfred Douglas in 1893.
- ✉ **Lover, Lover, Darling,** Signed by Zelda Sayre (1900–1948) to F. Scott Fitzgerald in the spring of either 1919 or 1920.
- ✉ **Always,** You could also try, "always" by itself. This is a favorite of mine—one simple word that says a great deal.
- ✉ **With (something),** With love, with admiration, with adoration, with endless devotion.
- ✉ **Love,** Simple, yet always effective.
- ✉ **Love and luck,** A cute way to end a platonic love letter. I saw this at the Country Music Hall of Fame—a Patsy Cline (1932–1963) letter on display. It was a one-and-a-half-page, handwritten letter to one of her fans. Now that's a grateful celebrity! On a side note, one of Patsy's albums was entitled *Sentimentally Yours* (1962).

Grammar

In love letters it is the words and the emotions supporting those words that are the stars of the show, so you're welcome to take grammatical liberties. Keep in mind that grammar is a tool used to make thoughts come across as clearly as possible and also to insert spoken-word inflections into the written word, so don't set grammar aside to the point where some of your sentiments are lost.

---

*Unless you're writing a love letter for someone who does not feel the same way. See Unauthorized Love Letters on page 68.

I once dated a man who would e-mail me and consistently misuse all of his homophones (words pronounced alike but different in spelling and meaning). He'd tell me he got stuck outside in the pooring rain, or he'd ask weather or not my interview went well. Truthfully, this boy blue my mind and I, of coarse, was so taken with him that I found his mistake absolutely adorable. So again, grammatical inconsistencies in love letters are easily forgiven and oftentimes endearing.

How to Send
Whether handwritten or typed, my vote here is that the letter ends up on paper—something to hold on to. I have no problem with typed letters because they'll take on a nostalgic charm of their own someday. I find old letters written via clunky typewriters as enchanting as a lover's poor penmanship. When it comes to delivery, the element of surprise is important. Slip it into a startling spot—the kitchen table, the lunch bag, the driver's seat. I think it'd be fun to hand it to them before they get in the shower. If you're away from your love for a while, then you have the perfect opportunity to do it the old-fashioned way and mail it. That being said, I fully understand that love lends to many out-of-control moments, so if you can't wait and you must send your sentiments immediately, then e-mail away. Who am I to stop love in motion?

If You Receive a Love Letter
Be grateful and enjoy. Certainly let your enthusiast know you received the letter and how much it means to you (I hear sexual favors are widely accepted as a thank-you), but I wouldn't return with a giant gesture right away. That implies that you're doing it because they did it first, and love letters are most effective when given out of the blue.

One very sweet moment in great 1980s cinema comes at the end of *Flashdance*—Nick is waiting outside for Alex after her big dance audition and hands her a bouquet of roses. She takes one of the flowers out of the bunch and hands it back to him. The moral here is, return a big gesture with a small one. Then wait your turn to surprise them with an equally moving love letter when they least expect it.

Great Expectations

'Tis true that I emphasize the element of surprise in giving love letters, but I realize that's impossible on certain occasions. There are designated days—Valentine's Day, birthdays, anniversaries, etc.—when your significant other is harboring high expectations for an amorous gesture. The good news is, there are infinite ways to put new twists on old words and actions. If you always deliver glorious gifts, then catch your love off guard by adding some length and thought to the card—or giving a card for the first time if you usually don't. If you're a frequent card giver then try highlighting a few details about the other person that you have noticed but never mentioned, or stress your favorite features in a way you never have before.

You could also resort to a humorous approach as my ex-boyfriend-still-very-good-friend, Jesse, did a few years ago. He bought me a 'You're a Nice Cousin' Card for Valentine's Day. It was clever and much appreciated. FYI: His nickname for me used to be "Noodle." Let there be no mystery to this nickname—I bear a striking resemblance to a long, skinny strand of pasta.

2/13/01

My Dearest Noodle,
I thought this card was hilarious. I bet they don't sell many "I love you cousin" cards on V. day, except maybe in West Virginia. Anyway, I am sitting here foolishly trying to capture my feelings for you in this card. If I had a thousand cousins in love cards, I couldn't describe my feelings for you.

I can only express to you that this has been the best year of my life. You are the most engaging person I have ever met.

You continue to impress me and make me fall in love with you every time we are together. I am closer to you than I have been with anyone on this earth. You are my best friend, lover, entertainment, obsession, solace, comfort, object of my most intense desire and owner of my heart. And for that, I will love you forever. Happy Valentine's Day!

Love always, Your *Jesse*

Crush Confessions

I've had a handful of people write me and say they're dating someone new and want to send a letter confessing their interest and intrigue but fear coming on too strong. Initially, this was difficult for me because I tend to play no-holds-barred when writing about feelings, but a little self-discipline never hurts. After enough of these requests I dubbed this type of letter the "crush confession." It's the little sister of the love letter—a breezy note telling that you're standing on comfortable ground and anticipate an onset of stronger feelings.

A good way to start these is to get it all out and write everything you feel. Yes, I said everything. Next, take out your red pen and edit away. Remove everything that fits into the "coming on too strong" category—be optimistic and save it for later. Then send along your watered-down declaration. The following crush confession is the summation of a few that I've written:

Dear Chris,

I wanted to drop you a quick note and come clean about something. I have admired you for all the time we've known each other, but I am really enjoying getting to know you in this new romantic context. One of my favorite things to do is be myself, and it's nice to spend time with someone who makes that so easy.

I look forward to hearing more of your travel stories and spending an obscene amount of time kayaking, which I'm so glad you enjoy as much as I do. You have such a welcoming air around you and I didn't want you to think it went unnoticed on my part. I know we're taking things slow, as we should because we've both been burned before, but I thought you might like to know how much fun I'm having.

Yours, *Karla*

If You Receive a Crush Confession

Crush confessions are great for a status check. If you're dating someone and they hand over one of these, then they're telling you that they think you're a good catch and are gearing up to move forward. If you receive a crush confession and feel the exact same way then I suggest you put this book down and go kayaking. If you do not feel the same way, it's courteous to tell them that—lest they fall any further. I know it seems obvious but all too often people are flattered by the idea that someone likes them and they think, *I'll see what happens,* rather than admit they don't share the same mind-set. Whoever wrote the letter gave you fair warning about their feelings and you should return the favor. If you decide to write your response to them it could go something like this:

Dear Karla,

Thank you so much for your very thoughtful note. You are absolutely the best kayaking partner I've ever had, and I too, have enjoyed our time together. That makes this more difficult to say, but I think you should know that I'm not on the exact same page as you. Our romantic endeavor crept up on me, and I wasn't fully prepared for all that it would entail. My uncertainty is not your problem, and I don't want it to become your problem. With that in mind I think it's best to put the brakes on this. I can explain further if you'd like, but I'd rather do so in person. If I've misled and disappointed you, I apologize.

Chris

Remember Mom

Don't reserve love letters solely for the people you love erotically, they equally affect the people you love platonically. And since love letters are seldom expected in a friend/family relationship, with the exception of special occasions, you're almost always guaranteed to catch them completely off guard when you deliver. The same rules in writing these love letters apply—obviously you're just going to leave the romance out.

I know a woman who writes letters in a journal to her young daughter. In the days leading up to the child's birth she expressed her uncontrollable enthusiasm about how she couldn't wait to meet her. Then she told her all the details of her birthday and what it was like to bring her home from the hospital. I imagine she keeps this going with big moments such as walking, talking, first day of school etc. And what a wonderful gift this book of letters will be to present to her daughter for sweet sixteen or graduation day.

My sister once surprised me with a love letter. We were sitting on the beach—I was reading and she was writing in her journal, or so I thought. As we walked back to the house she handed me a note. I had no idea what it was. Turns out, it was one of the most beautiful love letters I've ever received, and I'll cherish it always:

CIRCA 2000

To Whom It May Concern (Her birth name is Samara):
I have so many dreams and so much passion that I don't truly know how to express. Sometimes I think it's artistic passion, but I never really try to be artsy. Sometimes I think it's sexual passion, but you're my sister and that doesn't involve you. My basic point is that I want you to know you are an inspiration to me. Your honesty is refreshing, your inner beauty is inspiring, while your outer, breathtaking.

Although, speaking of honesty, I must admit at times I want to staple your mouth closed, but that is the joy of sisterhood. You are the only person in the world who shares my blood while caring enough to pick my brain for creative specks.

You know me, and not many people do. Thank you for that. For persevering through our younger days and achieving our current standing.

With hope and awe, *Lynn*

How to Confess Your Undying Love While You're Dying

BY JOHN KEATS (1795–1821)

Sketch of John Keats in 1918 by Charles Brown

Few literary legends ascended and descended as quickly as John Keats. A poetical prodigy, he posthumously earned his place among the fabulous five—Wordsworth, Coleridge, Byron, Shelley, Keats—poets of the Romantic Era (1785–1830). His first volume of poetry was published when he was twenty-two and his third and final when he was twenty-four—already suffering from the tuberculosis that would take his life a year later.

In 1818 he fell furiously in love with a young woman named Fanny Brawne—it has been noted that he wrote his best poetry between 1818 and 1819 when they were first courting. He wrote her more than three dozen letters, which she held on to until her death in 1865. It's remarkable that he was sick, well aware that he was dying and yet still able to muster up such a lively declaration of love:

13

MARCH 1820

Sweetest Fanny,

You fear, sometimes, I do not love you so much as you wish? My dear Girl I love you ever and ever and without reserve. The more I have known you the more have I lov'd. In every way—even my jealousies have been agonies of Love, in the hottest fit I ever had I would have died for you. I have vex'd you too much. But for Love! Can I help it? You are always new. The last of your kisses was ever the sweetest; the last smile the brightest; the last movement the gracefullest. When you pass'd my window home yesterday, I was fill'd with as much admiration as if I had then seen you for the first time. You uttered a half complaint once that I only lov'd your Beauty. Have I nothing else then to love in you but that? Do not I see a heart naturally furnish'd with wings imprison itself with me? No ill prospect has been able to turn your thoughts a moment from me. This perhaps should be as much a subject of sorrow as joy—but I will not talk of that. Even if you did not love me I could not help an entire devotion to you: how much more deeply then must I feel for you knowing you love me. My Mind has been the most discontented and restless one that ever was put into a body too small for it. I never felt my Mind repose upon anything with complete and undistracted enjoyment—upon no person but you. When you are in the room my thoughts never fly out of window: you always concentrate my whole senses. The anxiety shown about our Loves in your last note is an immense pleasure to me: however you must not suffer such speculations to molest you any more: nor will I any more believe you can have the least pique against me. Brown is gone out—but here is Mrs. Wylie—when she is gone I shall be awake for you.—Remembrances to your Mother.

Your affectionate, J. Keats

EROTIC LETTERS

I was tempted to call this the "lust letter" section because I'm a big fan of alliteration and that has an alluring sound, but I decided it's too misleading. Lust alone usually doesn't lend to substantial acts such as letter writing. It's a fleeting emotion—it reaches its boiling point quickly and evaporates soon after it's satisfied. It's unlikely you'd ever take the time to write a sexually charged letter for someone you only lusted after as these letters are filled with very personal and potentially embarrassing information that you'd only want someone you trusted to have access to. This is not to say lust is always a devious emotion—when it's accompanied by the melodious orchestra of love it finds a more meaningful and extended purpose.

It's a common assumption that love and lust are ardent enemies, and they are rarely recognized for working together and even keeping each other alive. After all, we must credit lust and desire for pushing us past the platonic point and encouraging us to take romantic interest in someone. Then once a relationship is established, love is what holds you together when lust takes one of her many leaves, and when love is at its most challenging sometimes a moment of unassigned passion can reignite your union.

The idea of love and lust working together as partners came together long ago in the Greek word eros, hence erotic, which literally means sexual love. In order to experience complete eros, you need to lust after the one you love. For married couples and long-term partners, sex is the relationship within the relationship that comes with its own set of joys and complications. If all is going well except for the sex then all isn't going well. On the flip side, if sex is the only link you have, then you don't have an authentic bond. Oftentimes if it was the thing that brought you together, it can also be the thing that drives you apart. It's easy to overlook the importance of sex because outside of a relationship it's readily misused, but on the inside it is the cornerstone connection. As time goes by this connection becomes more difficult, and therefore more important, to make.

Here's the part where letters can come in handy. Sex is tricky because while you want to get to a point where you know exactly what your lover likes, you don't want things to become so familiar that they're trite and routine. Putting your passions on paper is a great way to update your lover on your latest fantasies and to praise them for the many ways they please you. There are two types of erotic letters: The creation and the re-creation. The creation letter is the fantasy letter. You're telling your devoted one what you'd like to happen—what you saw in a movie or dreamed up in the doctor's office and can't wait to try. The re-creation is the exciting recollection of a successful sexual escapade you can't stop thinking about.

Truth be told, I've never written an entirely erotic letter—I've included erotic sentiments in love letters and also good-bye and break-up letters (hey, why not?). I include them here, however, for two reasons: 1) I think they're important. 2) I plan to write them. As I said, these types of letters tend to support relationships and I haven't been in one in longer than I care to admit. So the letter you are about to read is the only letter in this book that is completely fabricated. Since so much of sex is fantasy-based anyway, I'm hoping you'll let me get away with it.

Now for the fun part: The pseudonym for my pseudo man is Oliver. He's roughly 6'4" and has that killer dark brown hair/baby blue eyes combination and washboard abs (obviously). We'll meet running in Central Park one day. He'll be in town because he's teaching Atmospheric and Planetary Science at Columbia, which is what he does when he's between projects for NASA. Oh, I'm sorry, I must've gotten carried away.

Anyway . . .

The Erotic Letter

Oliver,

What got into you last night? Whatever it was I'm glad it got into me too. My hopes of a late night tryst fell asleep with you on the couch. I admitted defeat and headed to get ready for bed. Needless to say I was in a state of complex confusion as my dress went up, panties came down, and I found myself holding onto the headboard for dear life. I was the victim of a series of surprises—my favorite being when you insisted me on top of you and as I started to spread my legs you slid down quickly to lick me from beneath. As much as I loved when you did that I must admit I found it slightly (just slightly) more pleasurable when we switched places and you were on top, leaning back to play with my pussy while kneeling over and letting me suck on your sweetness. You know I never liked that position until I realized how much you enjoy the view. I imagine you like the noise too—my would-be moans muffled directly by your cock. It must sound like torture when I come.

And aren't you kind to note that one of my favorite places is standing and facing against the wall (like some naughty in-génue) where you can taunt so easily—leaving one hand free to do its will with my tender nipples and lucid clit while the other holds my hands high above my head and ensures my wrists are cinched and in a certain amount of pain. You took a while to relieve the pain last night—motioning to put your-self inside several times and deciding not to, knowing that I drip wetter and ache more—then and now—with every tease. I feared you might be gentle about it, but you sent me straight to my tiptoes and gasping for air when you finally did push yourself inside.

Afterwards I collapsed in exhaustion. This is my preferred

brand of exhaustion by the way, much better than the generic stuff. I'm meeting Julie after work for a drink. I won't be long.

Restlessly, *Samara*

Be Specific

It's easier to be specific with erotic letters then any other kind of letter because you're an expert on your own pleasure points and you strive to be an expert on your lover's. Now I know what comes so easily to the mind doesn't always translate to words. Some erotica reads like poetry and some reads like porn, it depends on what you and your partner prefer. A good way to start is by structuring your sentences around your senses:

- *Sight* "It's not that I don't love our frantic tumbles, but at some point I am going to insist that you stand in front of me and undress. Slowly. Painfully slow. So that I'm longing for you to do it faster as you politely refuse. Make my eyes drink down every section of your extraordinary body."

- *Sound* "Did I tell you how hot it was when you lowered your voice on the phone the other day? I know it was because people had walked in, but it turned me right on. Please do that more often. Lower your voice to a sexy whisper and tell me how hungry you are."

- *Smell* "It's hard to be in polite company when you have the scent of strawberries circling your neck—it makes me want to dig in and devour you."

- *Touch* "I lost my balance as soon as your hands started to explore. I closed my eyes and didn't care to resist being held captive by the warmth, the wetness, the pain, and, ultimately, the pleasure."

☙ *Taste* "I have been thirsty all day, craving just one lascivious lick of your savory skin. You are undoubtedly my favorite flavor."

Signing Off
Erotic letters can end the same way as love letters or not at all. James Joyce didn't sign his erotic letters other than his name. There is also no closing for the scandalous letters in *Penthouse Letters*. If you still want sum up the sexual sentiment try these:

✉ *Restlessly, Longingly, Passionately,* Some of my favorite adverbs.
✉ *Until next time, or until tonight, until tomorrow, until tomorrow morning, until next Thursday after work but before soccer practice,* Okay, I'll stop.

Grammar
The last thing anyone will care about when reading this is the placement of your commas and semicolons. I think you could even get away with not capitalizing the first word of every sentence. Spellcheck if you want (especially if you use words like lascivious) and then you're good to go.

How to Send
Like love letters, I think these are best left on pillows, nightstands, top of the laundry pile, and any other ordinary place that could use a dose of excitement. If you're writing a recreation letter regarding last night and want to send it off immediately, then e-mail it. However, I caution

you against sending these to a work e-mail account. Let Yahoo, Hotmail, and AOL have all the fun.

If You Receive an Erotic Letter

If it's the first erotic letter you've ever received it can be understandably awkward. Like sex itself, it's not always easy to be naked in front of someone for the first time, and reading something equally as unabashed might take some getting used to. Also though, as with sex, you will get used to it, and hopefully get to the point where you're willing to respond. Unlike love letters, I don't think there's a need for lag time here. Respond as soon as you like with a letter or, better yet, with the fantasy-come-true.

Describing "Down There"

Now comes the question what words are best to describe the act and the parts. The madame of erotic short stories, Anaïs Nin, often referred to a woman's womanly area simply as her "sex." As in "Then his hand slipped down to the little valley around the sex. I was growing lax and soft." I've always found something mysterious and poetic about that. She usually referred to a man's penis as his penis, but I think the use of the simple word *sex* could work there as well.

I lean toward mixing sweet analogies with inappropriate ones—the raunchy, raw words that when used out of context are made to insult and degrade. But we're not out of context here—we actually couldn't be more in context, and there's an undeniable pleasure in freely using words that have been deemed forbidden. If you can't disassociate these words with their degradation then fear not, there are other options:

> *Private Part Pronouns* You don't always have to name the specific body parts you're referring to. You could just name yourself or the other person and give a few other context

clues. For example, "I'd much rather you spend your afternoons deep inside me," or "I get excited at the mere thought of tasting you."

❡ *Forbidden Fruit*   Fruit is always a reliable and appropriate analogy. In her short story "The Queen" Anaïs Nin wrote, "Her nipples were hard like berries under the touch of the brush." Fruit acts as a perfect parallel, not only for breasts, but also for the look and taste of female lips—lips of the mouth as well as lips of the sex. There is a bit of a double standard here as it works well for describing the female genitalia—cherry, strawberry, apricot, peach, pear, pomegranate—but not so much the male. I can't describe the penis as a banana and be expected to keep a straight face. If you can, then a banana split it is.

❡ *Animal Instinct*   When we break it down, it's our sex drives that render us mere animals—making them a fitting comparison. Before we called it doggie style, James Joyce referred to it as "a hog riding a sow." King Solomon also relied on our friends in the animal kingdom for effective erotic descriptions, "Your breasts are like two fawns, twins of a gazelle, that feed among the lilies" (Song of Solomon 4:5).

❡ *Speaking of Solomon*   I'd like to give a shout out to an ancient king who used flora, fauna, and food to write luring erotica for his young bride: "You are stately as a palm tree and your breasts are like its clusters. I say I will climb the palm tree and lay hold of its branches. Oh may your breasts be like the cluster of the vine, and the scent of your breath like apples, and your kisses like the best wine that goes down smoothly gliding over lips and teeth" (Song of Solomon 7:7).

Position of Power

The good news is with these letters you have the power to cure your lover of certain self-consciousnesses. For example, in the movie *Bridget Jones: The Edge of Reason,* a naked Bridget gets out of bed and tries to get dressed with the covers still wrapped around her. Her beloved Mark Darcy asks her what she's doing and she says, "I don't want you to see my wobbly parts." He replies, "I happen to like your wobbly parts." She then proudly throws the cover to the floor. DIS-CLAIMER: Best not to use the expression "wobbly parts" unless you're British.

The bad news is you also have the power to make your lover more self-conscious. Be careful not to fantasize beyond what you know them to be capable of. For example, don't put pressure on them by saying (in a *creation* letter) something such as, "you lasted for well over an hour," or "you came in the missionary position." We all want certain things to happen but have little control over whether they can or will. Describe the setup in your letter, but not necessarily the finish, as that depends on so many things. Now if the setup and the finish go unexpectedly well, then be sure to celebrate that in a re-creation letter.

Also, try not to bring up a known point of contention like "I walked in one day, and I was so excited to find you watching porn!" If there's something you'd really like to try and your partner is severely opposed to it then you should discuss it. It's unhealthy for you to privately harbor a fantasy as it could manifest itself into you thinking you need outside sources to satisfy it. Try finding a variation that you're both comfortable with. It'd be irresponsible of your partner to completely ignore your fantasy, and it'd be irresponsible of you not to try and understand why they're uncomfortable with it. Ah, relationships.

Open Book

Here's my plan: Someday, if and when I'm married, I'm going to keep a journal of all my sordid fantasies. I will leave this journal wide open in obvious places for my husband to find and hopefully enjoy. I really only would do this with a husband, by the way, as I fear that with a boyfriend it might end up on the Internet in the event of a bad breakup. Also, it's not something I feel we would necessarily need in the early years but perhaps the later ones. I'll write to a third-person party to make him feel as though he really has stumbled upon something he shouldn't be reading. I think I'll write to the young Brigitte Bardot. I imagine the Parisian beauty would like nothing more than to sit in her ivory tower and advise me on my sex life. Once aforementioned husband has all the information, he is welcome to fulfill my fantasies at his own will, and he is certainly more than welcome to write back and include his own.

I share my plan with you in case you'd like to use it. I like the idea of the journal playing middleman because, while experts emphasize that you have to communicate to your partner what you do and don't want, there's still a part of all of us that just wants our lover to know what we want without us saying anything. This is one way to accomplish that. Write your desires down, forget about them and one day they just might come true. As sexual beings we evolve. We change. Things that once repulsed us now intrigue and excite—always a good idea to let your lover be the first to know about such developments.

How to Undress Your Lover
With Your Words

BY JAMES JOYCE (1882-1941)

A portrait of the artist as a young man—twenty-two-year-old James Joyce in 1904
Photograph courtesy of SUNY Buffalo

Writing this biographical section is bittersweet for me. Bitter because I cannot show you the letters that I'd like, and sweet because what's keeping me from reprinting these erotic epistles is the fact that that letters are alive and well and still causing controversy. I wasn't sure exactly what my search for historic erotic letters would yield. It ended up yielding a set of early twentieth-century letters so graphic they could easily offend and perturb early twenty-first-century readers.

One day whilst surfing the net, I came across some steamy missives supposedly written by James Joyce. Joyce, born in Ireland, is often referred to as the greatest writer of the twentieth century—his major works include *Ulysses* (1922) and *Finnegans Wake* (1939). I was skeptical as to whether the letters were real or not, so I hauled over to library, sat Indian-style on the floor, and thumbed anxiously through *The Selected Letters of James Joyce*. I was thrilled to find they were not only real but really explicit. Every obscenity made an appearance—oral sex (standard and 69), anal sex (he was delighted to discover she liked it "arseways") the F word, the C word, and a few disturbing fetishes. The best part: These are love letters. They were written to a woman named Nora Barnacle who Joyce had met and fallen in love with in 1904. Five years later, in 1909, the two were living in Trieste, Italy, with two children. In October of that year, Joyce went to Dublin for business and while still away in December he and Nora began the erotic exchange (again, they're writing these five years and two children into their relationship). Her letters were never found, but it's clear from his letters that she was fully on board. These letters are somewhat unsettling—this is the risk you take when indulging someone else's erotica—and yet a magnificent union of love and lust. For every potentially offensive sentiment—and there are many—there is an extraordinary sentiment to bring her (and us) back to the reality of his love. On December 2, 1909 he wrote:

> But, side by side and inside the spiritual love I have for you there is also a wild beast like craving for every inch of your body, for every secret and shameful part of it, for every odour and act of it. My love for you allows me to pray to the spirit of eternal beauty and tenderness mirrored in your eyes or fling you down under me on that softy belly of yours and fuck you up behind, like a hog riding a sow, glorying in the very stink and sweat that rises from your arse, glorying in the open shape of your upturned dress and white girlish drawers and in the confusion of your flushed cheeks and tangled hair.

Joyce himself once said of these salacious letters, nine published in total, "Some of it is ugly, obscene and bestial, some of it is pure and holy and spiritual: all of it is myself."

As you can see, these letters are well-equipped to offend modern eyes, and they do. Namely, they offend the eyes of James and Nora's grandson, Stephen Joyce, who now oversees his grandfather's estate. Joyce holds a rigid right hand over both the literature and letters in his domain. The James Joyce Estate has been known to stop public readings of *Ulysses* and wreak havoc at James Joyce exhibits all in the name of copyright infringement.

In 2004, another one of the December 1909 erotic letters, thought to be lost for good, was found and auctioned off at Sotheby's in London for the equivalent of $445,000—four times the expected price. The estate would not release the content of the letter, making it clear that this letter was not meant for publication. I tend to think if you're willing to nominate yourself for literary immortality, as James Joyce did, then you freely place your privacy on the ledge knowing it could fall off it at any moment. I also think Stephen Joyce is not protecting his grandfather's privacy but rather his own. He doesn't want to be the kid on the playground when all the other kids know his grandpa wrote some dirty letters.

The bad news is that all letters written to Nora are off limits for reproduction. The good news is they are sitting silently on library shelves across the country, as they have been since 1976 (Stephen Joyce says they were published originally behind his back). The built-in irony is that James Joyce spent much of his literary career being censored. *Ulysses* was banned in both the United States and the United Kingdom for—you'll never guess what—lewd sexual content. Copyright on all of James Joyce's letters expires in 2012—my watch is set. Despite knowing the odds of Stephen Joyce allowing me to reprint any of these letters were next to none, I still had to try:

My Letter to Stephen Joyce

MAY 5, 2006

Dear Mr. Joyce,

I hope this letter finds you well. I have a request of you and I am almost certain you will not rule in my favor, but I hope you can appreciate my need to ask. I also hope you are willing to read this letter in its entirety.

I am currently writing a book about letter writing, and I plan to empha-size how this practice needs to be carried out well into the twenty-first century and beyond—lest we as early twenty-first-century regulars risk leaving no evidence of our existence and practices. I am including a handful of historical letters in this book to create a live connection between yesterday and today. It gives people, myself especially, great comfort to know that the emotions that rule our lives—such as love, lust, anger, determination, and frustration— have ruled the lives of individuals since the beginning. We tend to forget this and convince ourselves that their lives were somehow easier and more ethical, when in many cases their lives were much more difficult and their ethics remarkably askew.

I have compiled a list of letters—including those written by John Keats, Edgar Allan Poe, Susan B. Anthony, and Abraham Lincoln—and would very much like to include a letter by James Joyce. The letter I have in mind was written to Nora Barnacle on December 2, 1909. It is to my understanding that the letters written to Nora in December of that year are a sensitive subject as they are of an erotic nature. I find them to be a magnificent juxtaposition of love and lust. These letters serve to show how two people were able to keep their passion alive and well five and half years into their relationship. They also illustrate a man's ability to project both his animal instincts and intellectual love onto one woman. And, obviously, they are remarkably well written.

I first came across these letters on the Internet and the site showed the letters in fragments. I wasn't sure if they were real or not, so I explored further and found that they were. To my disappointment, what the Web site had done was cut out all evidence of love and left only erotic sentiments. I fear that when the copyright on Joyce's work expires in 2012 that that is how these letters will be passed around and perceived. It will go unmentioned that the woman he was writing to was the love of his life and the mother of his children.

I can imagine it isn't easy for you to think of your grandparents in such a way, but you've also had to make many concessions with their notoriety that the rest of us haven't had to. I beseech you; please let me reintroduce these as the brilliant, brazen love letters that they are. I am more than willing to have you approve the text that will precede the December 2nd letter.

I know that the stance of the Estate is that this is not Joyce's literary work and therefore is not a subject of general interest. If you'll allow me to disagree— intimate human relations undoubtedly intrigues all people, and I think it certainly qualifies as general interest. The Selected Letters of James Joyce *was published based on the assumption that people craved a more personal look at this extraordinary writer.*

I'm sure you'd rather these letters had never been published, which is understandable. But that is not the issue at hand as they already have been, and I believe abating their reproduction is in the same vein as banning Ulysses— *as it once was both in the United States and United Kingdom. James Joyce certainly let his life influence his literature and he let his literary style influence his letters. I believe that letters are literature and would very much like to see James Joyce live on uncensored. Please consider this. Thank you for your time.*

Kind regards, *Samara O'Shea*

His Response

I didn't hold out high hopes that he would get back to me, but he put me to shame—not only did he reply, he handwrote his response. As expected, he basically told me to go to Hell, but he took an appreciated ten minutes out of his life to do it. If you'd like to view the letter he wrote me, it's posted on my Web site: LetterLover.net.

2   Letter Therapy

I'm gonna sit right down and write myself a letter
and make believe it came from you.
—Joe Young / Fred E. Alhert

One of the lesser-known benefits of letter writing is how well you can get to know yourself in the process. In order to accurately explain to someone else what's going on within, you first need to have your own firm grasp of it. When speaking, we often tell others what we think they want to hear or what comes conveniently, sometimes irrationally to mind. When writing, you set aside quality time with yourself and end up examining your relationship with the soon-to-be receiver. Before delivering the message you'll confirm that, yes, this is in fact how I feel. Sometimes seeing your thoughts out in the open offers a consolation in itself, and you realize it was you and not them who needed the clarification. Other times you can reread what you wrote and thank God you never sent it because it was written hastily and in a moment of fleeting anger. Herein lies the solace some people get from keeping a diary or journal.

In the same vein as personal insight, letters also act as a vessel of closure. The meaning of emotional closure varies from situation to situation—ultimately it's whatever enables you to end one chapter in your life and start the next. When an act of closure cannot or does not come from the person who can grant it, letters can help you create your own and move on.

Although good-bye letters and flaming-tongue (angry) letters seem a far cry from each other, I include them together because they are the two types of letters that can be emotionally advantageous whether they are sent or unsent.

GOOD-BYE LETTERS

Good-bye letters are communicative chameleons. They adapt to their surroundings and can make sense in several situations. The only absolute sentiment that they have to convey is "farewell," but the details after that can vary. For example, they could be breakup type letters, as in: Good-bye I never want to see you again. They could be "break" letters: Good-bye, let's meet up again a few months from now when we both have our heads on straight. They could be love letters: Farewell for now, until we meet again. In any case, they offer a sense of finality. They close the door behind your time spent with one person and open the door to life that's a little, and sometimes a lot, different.

There's something incredibly human about saying good-bye. A missed opportunity to do so is often met with deep disappointment. I know a handful of people who have written letters and placed them in a casket. It made them feel better as they were unable to say good-bye to the deceased. Sometimes initiating a difficult good-bye can be a personal triumph—it is both devastating and empowering when you admit to yourself that a friend, lover, or even family member is hurting you too much and it's in your best interest to walk away. The Billy Joel song "Stop in Nevada" tells the story of a woman emotionally estranged from her husband, who makes the sudden, seemingly necessary decision to leave: "Now she's headed out to California. It's been a long time coming but she's feeling like a woman tonight. And she left a little letter says she's gonna make a stop in Nevada. Good-bye."

I've written good-bye letters of all kinds. I'll discuss this more in regard to letters of gratitude (a few chapters away), but I find when leaving a job or other temporary state of affairs a combination good-bye/thank you missive is much appreciated by those left behind. It's something people tend to remember. Of course the most memorable of my good-bye letters have been in the end-of-the-affair arena. I believe there's a difference between breakup and good-bye letters. A breakup letter is usually the beginning of the end—you're officially announcing that the relationship is over but there's a call for some back and forth. A good-bye letter is given when all is said and done—it's clear that things haven't worked out and, for what's it's worth, you hand over your final thoughts. A good-bye letter can also make it clear that you're out no matter what, and things aren't open for discussion at all, as it did in Lady Nevada's case.

This good-bye letter falls under the "small personal feat" category— the whole process felt like taking a deep breath. I'd say I was dating a man but we never really made it to the dating part. How about I say we knew each other socially, we e-mailed a lot, and went out once. After that date we exchanged a few follow-up e-mails and then he disappeared. I was undoubtedly disappointed but not entirely surprised as I sensed his hesitation. Fast-forward two months; he e-mailed me what was, for the most part, a very nice apology letter (see letter, page 102). I didn't want to be but I was very happy to hear from him. We eased back into a virtual repartee, which amounted to him saying he'd do anything to redeem himself. For fun, I listed a number of humiliating tasks and two real ones. Humiliating tasks: 1) Spend a week in Robin Hood–inspired tights. 2) Go Brad Pitt blond. 3) Make out with several men of my choice. Real tasks: 1) Call me. 2) Be prepared to trek to my neighborhood (a very inconvenient stone's throw from his). He wittingly entertained the shameful errands for a while and was willing to do the neighborhood thing, but not the calling thing.

Now, had this been back in those dark days before the book *He's Just Not That Into You* (Simon & Schuster, 2004) came to save women from themselves, I may not have noticed. But it's rule number #2: He's Just Not That Into You If He's Not Calling that came into play, and it was fascinating to watch. He would tell me he'd love to talk me, and then he wouldn't call. He told me this great story about losing my cell phone number; meanwhile my work number appears at the bottom of every e-mail I send. I am obviously a fan of the written word, but not so much that it trumps the spoken word, especially when acts of redemption are concerned.

After days of going back and forth and him ignoring my request, I sighed in defeat, but this time I walked away. I had already been cast off once and didn't want to set myself up to have it happen again. Let me say this: It is beyond therapeutic. It is emotionally emancipating to look at someone and say, "I like you. I like you sooooo much, but there is one person here I have to like more than I like you and that is me." (Greg Behrendt* are you reading this? Aren't you proud of me?!)

The Good-bye Letter

From: Samara@emailprovider.com
To: Mr.Indecisive@emailprovider.com
09/30/05 11:39 AM
I'm sorry, but I'm not doing this. Actually, I'm not sorry I'm not doing this, it's just a slightly more polite way to start off such a sentence. It is poor form for you to boast that you'll do anything (in caps even) to redeem yourself and not be willing to pick up the telephone and end this cyberspace charade. It's not that I don't enjoy e-mailing with you. I love the directions our banters tend to go in, but I don't need a pen pal.

The refrain you kept reciting over the summer was "I don't know what I want." My advice to you: There's only one thing you need to know when you're dating someone, and that is

---

*Coauthor of *He's Just Not That Into You*.

that you can't wait to see them again. Yes, I believe it's that's simple. You leave their presence and think, "Wow, when can I see them again?" If it's any more complicated than that, then it's too complicated. And I have wondered, "When can I see him again?" since the day I met you. I have no shame in saying such a thing, as it's never been a secret here that my interest outweighed yours. If I don't evoke similar sentiments in you, then there's no need to waste either of our time. We both agree it's nothing short of a miracle for two people to stand on the exact same level of interest and attraction, so I'm not offended. I completely understand.

I don't want this to undermine your apology. You apologized, and I genuinely appreciate it. Consider your karma clear. I just don't see the need to take it any farther than that.

All the best to you,
Samara

Be Specific

The two issues every good-bye letter should address are where you're going and why you're going there. They should also touch upon whether you're planning to come back or not. If you're not physically going away but rather ending a relationship, then you should explain your metaphorical leave of absence. In good-bye/love letters you can gush about not wanting to leave and how much you'll miss the other person.

> *How to Start*   Tell them where you're coming from. If you've come to this conclusion after a long time: "I've thought this through, and this is something I have to do" or if it was a more sudden decision: "This is going to catch you off guard. It caught me off guard also, but it feels like the right thing to do." If you're writing a good-bye/love letter, start off with something along the lines of "I'm going to miss you so much."

 Good-bye Forever Trying to convey this is easier than you think, and yes, you can do it without being cruel. Sometimes relationships, whether romantic or not, have to end with no one at fault. It's either a classic clash of personalities or simply two people wanting very different things from each other—as was the case above. You can say directly, "This needs to be our last contact as I've already thought about this countless times," or you can imply it with words that don't lend themselves to future contact. Ending a letter with "I wish you well in all that you do" aids in getting that message across.

 Good-bye for Now A "break" is an acceptable and well-known chapter in many relationships and even some friendships. In letters referring to this, you'll want to make it clear that you do hope to get back in touch; you just need space for the time being: "I look forward to reconvening with you perhaps later this year, but for now I need time to think things through."

 Distance Drama If you're ending an otherwise good relationship because of a distance situation that is imminent and irrevocable, then make sure you distinguish that as being the barrier between you: "Please don't doubt for a second that you are the object of my full affection and in any other circumstance I would be wholly yours. Since our lives can't have us any closer and it doesn't seem like they'll be able to accommodate us for years—if ever—I think it's best that we not strain ourselves with a long-distance relationship."

 Lasting Words of Love I think temporary separations, more so than almost any other situation, lend to extraordinary love letters—as the cliché "absence makes the heart grow fonder" tends to be true. For this, follow basic rules in the love letter chapter and throw in some good-bye sentiments such as, "This time apart is going to kill me, but if it has to be then I am looking forward to craving you each and every moment I'm gone."

⟡ **Upon My Return**   Consider ending good-bye/love letters with a "when I get back" segment. This is the perfect time to embellish a new fantasy or simply make the point that you'll spend a great deal of time together on the other side of the trip.

Signing Off

✉ *I part with you in peace,*   Author of *A Vindication of the Rights of Women* and mother of Mary Shelley (think *Frankenstein*), Mary Wollstonecraft (1759–1797) wrote a harsh but necessary good-bye letter to fellow writer and lover Gilbert Imlay when his unfaithfulness reached its peak. Toward the end of the letter, she calmed down and ended it in this mature fashion.

✉ *Good-bye. I no longer believe. I no longer hope. I no longer love,*   French courtesan and proud bisexual Liane de Pougy (1869–1950) wrote this to the first great female love of her life, Natalie Barney, as their relationship was turning sour. Liane went on to write a book about the affair entitled *The Sapphic Idyll* (1901).

✉ *I bid you an affectionate farewell,*   On April 10, 1865, confederate army general, Robert E. Lee (1807–1870), having already surrendered to Ulysses S. Grant, wrote a farewell letter to his army.

✉ *I wish you well in all that you do,* and *All the best to you,*   I've found these to be kind, effective ways to end good-bye letters.

Grammar

If it's a good-bye/love letter you're writing, then you can let the grammar lapse. Any other type of good-bye letter, especially if you intend to be firm should be as clean as possible. Misspellings and poor punctuation can detract from conveying a strong message.

How to Send

Paper is most effective in conveying a strong sense of "the end." I know I've already broken my own rule (with Mr. Indecisive). The only problem with e-mail is it's very easy for the other person to reply, so if you really don't want any more contact, then you have to be very clear. Mine worked well—he never responded. If it's a good-bye/love letter you're writing, then let it be the last thing you hand the other person before they get in the car, on the plane, bus, or train. Of course you'll be in contact via phone and e-mail throughout your separation, but a paper letter is an extra-special good-bye gift.

Closure: A Melodramatic Analogy

As I said, I think good-bye letters can play a key role in giving both parties closure. Truth be told, I have no idea what closure is. I can offer no psychoanalysis as to where it comes from or why we need it. I do know that when a situation lacks closure—when I haven't had final words with someone—it sits itself in the back of my mind and hangs out for an undisclosed amount of time. I don't enjoy leaving doors ajar like that. I prefer to say good-bye.

Often, part of saying good-bye means having your questions answered—as we crave knowledge of every character's motivation in a novel, play, or movie, we also wish to know the incentives of the ever-changing cast in own lives. Whether it's the end of a friendship or romantic rendezvous, the first question we all ask is "Why?" usually followed by "How did this happen?" Chances are if you aren't asking those questions or don't feel a certain craving for closure, you can bet the other person needs it from you.

Now we move into my over-the-top analogy. I've chosen two androgynous names for this to avoid showing favoritism to either sex. I've heard just as many men cry, "Why couldn't she give me closure?" as I have heard women whimper the reverse. Read this however you'd like: Taylor and Alex have been together for little over a year now, and one day Taylor takes out a knife and slices Alex's arm open with it. Taylor then runs away. When Taylor gets to the corner, there's two choices waiting: 1) Keep running. 2) Turn around and help Alex. The difference from where Alex stands is this: Taylor cannot undo the sudden, mortal combat wound but can come back, stop the bleeding, wrap the gash, and then go. This way Taylor has helped Alex's healing begin. Now Alex may have a while before the injury is completely healed, but the point is it's on its way. Otherwise Alex is left alone with the bloody mess and there's no telling when the bleeding will stop—the process is at least doubled in length. Alex can opt to push Taylor away and refuse the aid, which still leaves Alex to deal with the problem alone. The melodramatic moral of the story is: You hurt someone or you got hurt yourself—you can't make the pain stop but you can get the healing started. This is closure.

A Tale of Two Letters

Now how do you obtain a sense of closure when the other party is unwilling to participate? I'm glad you asked. It's tough to take when you want to talk something through and the other person is content ignoring you, so in this situation it's best to try and create your own closure. I've successfully done this a few times and will tell you about two.

I once had a frowned-upon relationship with a coworker. It didn't end well and, after it didn't end well, it got worse as he would bring the girl he was dating to work and parade her around. Being ignored is one thing. Being ignored by a person you have to see every day is excruciating. He wouldn't let me get close enough to call a truce. It was when I stopped trying that things became somewhat civil again and we were able to suffer small talk. Shortly thereafter, he announced he got a new job and would be leaving. A few days before his last day I found myself up late writing him a letter. It was a story of a letter—illustrating us. I didn't include any pretenses of future contact and ultimately wished him well. When I was done I felt this incredible feeling: the need not to give it to him. I had summed it up nicely for myself and that seemed to be enough. I coasted through the next few shifts with no discomfort whatsoever. On his last night I did bring the letter with me—before I left my apartment, the writer in me shouted, *Why would you write something someone else wasn't going to read?* I wasn't sure I was going to give it to him up until I actually did. I was getting ready to leave and knew I could hand it over and escape without a reaction. That plan failed miserably as the manager kept me longer than expected, and I ran into him on my way out. I could tell by the way he was smirking at me that he had read the letter. I held my breath. He walked by me and whispered that it was the nicest thing anyone had ever done for him. I'm sure I wrinkled my brow in candid confusion. Needless to say I was glad I gave it to him, but closure for me came the moment I realized I didn't have to.

I equate a lack of closure with a lack of control, and writing letters offers an opportunity to regain control of your own emotional state. The other letter that came through for me was one I really didn't send. I was dating a man for a little more than a month and he just stopped calling one day. It was a short time, yes, but I liked him a lot. I was in shock as this was my first experience with having a man disappear entirely—I have since become an expert on that predicament. I cracked open my journal one day and drafted a long good-bye letter to him. I reread it a few days later and realized I actually didn't need to send it at all. What I did send was a book he had let me borrow. I'm sure he didn't care to have it back, but I sent it anyway with a short note that said, "Thank you for this. It was nice meeting you." Technically he ended it, but something about having confessed all to my journal and then having the literal last word made me feel as if I had participated in the finale and therefore obtained closure.

How to Say Good-bye Before
Going to the Guillotine

BY MARIE ANTOINETTE (1755–1793)

Fifteen-year-old Marie Antoinette, painted by Franz Xavier Wagenschon

Born into Austrian royalty, Maria Antonia Josefa Joanna von Habsburg-Lothringen, was married to the French Dauphin Louis-Auguste (later Louis XVI, 1754–1793) at the age of fourteen and thenceforth known as Marie Antoinette. She was crowned queen at the age of nineteen and is perhaps best known for allegedly uttering a callous comment about letting her subjects eat cake (there is little evidence to support her actually saying this). She and her husband reigned for sixteen years, then in 1789 the French Revolution initiated the end of absolute monarchism in France. A mob descended on the palace in Versailles and moved the members of the monarchy to Paris where they lived as prisoners for four years. Louis went to the guillotine in late January 1793, and Marie, nine months later. She wrote her last letter, to her sister-in-law Elisabeth, around 4 A.M.—eight hours before her execution. I imagine in the dark morning hours when you know dawn will bring your death, sleep isn't really an option, and writing the hopes for your children and making your peace with God would help prepare you mentally. Around eleven that same morning, she was paraded with her hands bound behind her back in a slow-moving cart around the streets of Paris for an hour before arriving at the Place de la Revolution for the beheading. She is said to have gone to the guillotine with a dignity that enraged her enemies.

OCTOBER 16, 1793, 4:32 IN THE MORNING

It is to you, my sister, that I write for the last time. I have just been
condemned, not to a shameful death, that is only for criminals, but to rejoin

your brother. Like him, I am innocent, I hope to show the same firmness in my last moments. I am calm, as one is when one's conscience does not reproach one. I feel a profound sadness in leaving my children. You know that I existed only for them; and you, my good and tender sister, you who have in your friendship sacrificed everything to be with us, in what a position I leave you!

I learned during the trial that my daughter was separated from you, alas the poor child, I do not dare write her, she would not receive my letter. I do not even know if it will reach you. Receive my blessings for you both; I hope that one day when they are grown older they will be reunited with you and enjoy your tender care. They must always remember what I never ceased to teach them, that principles and attention to duty are the foundation of life, that their friendship and trust will be its happiness. My daughter must think that since she is older she must always help her brother by the advice which her fuller experience and his love will inspire her, that they may feel in whatever situation they may find themselves they are only really happy in their union, that they follow our example and remember how through all our troubles our friendship has consoled us, and in happiness we have enjoyed it doubly because we have shared it with a friend, and where can one find the most tender and faithful friends if not in one's own family? And my son must never forget his father's last words, which I now solemnly repeat to him, that he should never seek to avenge our death. I have to speak to you of something which much afflicts my heart. I know how much this child has wounded you, pardon him, my dear sister, consider his age and how easy it is to make a child say what one will, and specially something he does not understand. A day will come I hope when he will feel more keenly what all your goodness and tenderness have been and what it cost you. It remains only for me to confide to you my last thoughts. I wished you to do this before the trial, but partly because they did not allow me to write and its progress was so rapid I really did not have the time.

I die in the Catholic Faith, Apostolic and Roman; that of my fathers, in which I was brought up and which I have always professed; having no consolation to hope for, not knowing if indeed there are still the priests of Faith and if there were whether it would not be too dangerous to come even to this place. I ask God's pardon for all the faults which I may have committed since I was born; I have no hope but in His goodness. I hope that in His mercy He will receive my last prayer and those which I have made so long, that He will receive my soul in His merciful kindness. I ask pardon of all whom I have known and in particular from you, my sister, for all the trouble which without meaning to I may have caused. Forgive all my enemies the evil they have done to me. I say good-bye to my aunts and to all my brothers and sisters. I had some friends. The thought of being separated from them is one of the greatest regrets I have in dying. They may know at least, that until my last moment I have thought of them.

Farewell, my good and tender sister, I hope that this letter may reach you. Do not forget me. I embrace you with all my heart as well as my poor children. My God! How it tears my heart to leave them forever. Farewell, farewell! I must now think of my spiritual duties. As I am not free they will perhaps bring me a priest (having taken the oath) but I swear here that I will not speak one word, and I will treat him as an absolute stranger.

Marie Antoinette

FLAMING-TONGUE LETTERS

Anger is a decisive emotion, which can be both good and bad. The good is you don't wait or waver—you say what's on your mind, you act instinctively, and there is no hesitation. I call this good because oftentimes problems that fester inside us wouldn't see the light of day save for intense moments of anger. Anger gives us permission to say just about anything. Anger is also a way to reinforce how serious or upset you are to whoever's present. We all know what the downside is—you don't think before you speak or act and can end up really hurting someone.

Anger in excess is never good, but in moderation it—like every emotion—plays a needed role in our lives. It was once a common assumption made by me and a few other family members that my cousin Jennifer and her husband (stars of the love letter chapter) never fought. That fight scene is really difficult to imagine. I asked her about it once and she said of course they fight and she'd wonder about a couple that never fought because that would signify that they didn't communicate. Differences are inevitable; it's how you handle them that counts.

Anger in letters—like anger in life—also teeters on the balance beam between good and bad. It's bad if you write when you're blind with rage and hand it over without a second thought. However, if you write when you're angry and edit when you're collected, then you can master the art of saying what needs to be said but communicating it in a way that's not so irrational you risk hurting someone beyond repair. I wrote this next letter for a friend who was furious with another friend of hers who I only knew in passing. She asked me to work on it because she knew I could write a more levelheaded letter. I was equipped to do this because I understood the story but wasn't suffering the same aggravation as she. The issue at hand centered around the timeless problem of having a friend who cannot juggle an old friendship and a new relationship.

The Flaming-Tongue Letter

(All names in this letter have been changed)

MAY 2004

Krista,
Needless to say I'm hurt but I'm not surprised. Your not showing up at my birthday party was an added injury to an already fading friendship. I am infuriated, with myself as well as you, for pretending everything was okay the day we spoke on the phone. Small talk was clearly the tool you used to avoid the problems at hand, and I was in shock that you were content to act as if everything was normal so I didn't speak my mind in time. Now I wish I had.

It hurts me so much that you haven't taken the time to ac-
knowledge we're having problems. I think Jake is the only
person you not only see but consider, and I think it's a shame
our relationship has to suffer because you haven't learned the
balancing act of life. This involves making time for friends
and family as well as your boyfriend and being able to enjoy the
company of each together as well as separately. I'm sorry you
feel the need to consult Jake on everything and deny yourself
even the slightest bit of independence. I know my relationship
with Carl has its problems, but one thing he and I both understand is that our friendships are nonnegotiable.

I know work was a nightmare for you, but I'm glad it brought
us together—even if only for a short time. I'll miss our late-
night gab sessions and *Sex in the City* marathons. I still hold a
small hope that we can salvage this, but that's up to you. I feel
as if I've done all I can at this point.

Holly

Be Specific

The good thing about writing angry letters is you don't have to put
much thought into them—everything will come to you, even things
you didn't know you were thinking. And again, the downside is because you don't put too much thought into them, you'll need to go
back and rethink them.

> *How to Start* Your anger will usually inspire you to get right
> to the point and state the reason you're angry, hurt, etc. If
> you're having trouble, another way to open is by giving the
> other person a frame of reference for the specific incident or
> the mounting problem. "I've tried and honestly cannot under-
> stand why you were so cold to me at Angela's dinner party," or
> "For a while now I've hoped your busy schedule was a phase,
> and time for us was right around the corner. It has become
> painfully clear that is not the case."

Sleep on It   Never send the first draft of an angry letter. By all means write it when you're fuming, then set it aside and read it the next day or when you've felt yourself calm down. When you edit, remove all the upper cuts and low blows. Keep the core—the thing that really upset you. The thing you need an apology for or the thing that has to be worked on in order for the relationship to survive. In waiting it's also possible to realize that you reacted too quickly and since you're seeing more clearly now, you might be able to throw away the letter and call it a day.

It Hurts Me   Don't write a laundry list telling the other person everything they do wrong—this will put them on the defensive. It's more effective to tell them how their actions affect you—they can't argue with how you feel. Rather than saying "You're so condescending," try "It hurts me when you make it sound as though your job is harder than mine."

Reverse Apology   Apologize to them for their behavior. For example, "I'm sorry you find it necessary to treat me this way." If you want to throw in a little sarcasm (remember, everything in moderation) you can try apologizing for your assets. As in, "I'm sorry I let my patience get the better of me." Be careful with the latter though—you don't want to go overboard, as in "I'm sorry I'm such a wonderful person." That's not necessary.

Easy on the Expletives   As the wit master himself, Mark Twain, once said, "When angry, count a hundred; when very angry, swear." I don't recommend riddling the entire letter with expletives—they'll lose their effectiveness if there's too many—but one or two in the name of emphasis is okay. A friend of mine once started an angry letter to another friend of ours with: "First of all: Fuck you." I thought it was brilliant, well worded, and well deserved as I had witnessed the clash that caused the letter. This way the initial anger was out on the table and the remainder of the letter was firm but not flaming.

Assert Your Worth Now is not the time to be humble or shy. The reason you're irate is because you're feeling undervalued. Someone is ignoring one or many of your needs. I was once in a verbal argument with a friend and she looked at me and said shamelessly, "Do you know what a good friend I am?" She was absolutely right to ask me that. If you feel someone is taking advantage of your good graces, feel free to remind them that you are a great person and they best treat you as such. You can find a prime example of this at the end of the chapter under Angry Letters Aloud.

Filter Through a Friend If you want the issue dealt with immediately and don't have time to sleep on it, consider showing the letter to a trusted friend first. They can help you gauge whether it's right on or needs revising.

Wish Them Well If the angry letter could result in the end of the relationship, as the example did, I wouldn't write it unless you can legitimately wish the other person well. Letters are permanent and, if the other person chooses to keep your letter, you don't want your last words to be damning them to Hell. You can tell them how distraught you are and still round out at the end to say what upsets you the most is that the relationship has taken a turn for the worse and you wish them the best, regardless.

Signing Off

Angry letters don't usually end with a two- or three-word sentiment, but oftentimes a strong sentence and simply signing your name. If you do choose to end with a traditional closing, I think it's best to make it a respectful one such as "yours" or "sincerely," as anger tends to be fleeting. These, on the other hand, are strong sentence endings:

- ✉ *It depends upon yourself if hereafter you see or hear from me.*
- ✉ *I have made every exertion but in vain.*
- ✉ *For God's sake pity me and save me from destruction.*   All of the above are from Edgar Allan Poe to his foster father, John Allan (more on these two at the end of this chapter).
- ✉ *Just leave me alone, if you don't want me to stop trusting you for good.*   In addition to her world-renowned diary, Anne Frank (1929–1945) also wrote letters while her and her family were in hiding. This heated sentence was part of a two-page letter written to her father, Otto, after he forbade her to be alone in the attic with the young son of the family with whom they were hiding.

Grammar

When writing these through a stream of angry consciousness, grammar will undoubtedly fall to the wayside. If you choose to reread to make sure your anger isn't too out of line before you send, then that's a good time to double-check your grammar. The cleaner it is, the stronger your point will be.

How to Send

It depends on the reality of seeing the person. If you live with them and can put it in a place you know they'll get it, then do that. If you're not speaking, then you can mail it. I only suggest e-mail if you're willing to turn your computer off and walk away once you're done writing. If you send the message and you're both in front of the screen, you could get into a heated match online. Nothing is worse than fighting over e-mail—there is ample room for misinterpretation. If you get into a virtual spat, one of you needs to step back and say, "We have to talk in person about this."

If You Receive a Flaming-tongue Letter

Try not to react hastily—read it once, then read it again a while later. Consider the other person's point of view. Remember that they're hurt and whether you intended to cause that pain or not, you need to think about what you can do to remedy the situation if you care to maintain the relationship. There should be a balance here—you'll probably spot at least a few details that make you want to defend yourself, but hopefully there'll also be particulars that you're willing to concede on. This is the essence of compromise. You can write back if you're not speaking to each other, but it's best to meet and discuss. If you see absolutely nothing wrong with what you've said or done, then it usually means one of three things: 1) There was a vast misunderstanding. 2) The person who wrote you is of little or no consequence to you. 3) You need to have your head examined. FYI: The apology letter section begins on page 96.

Angry Letters Aloud

One of the more effective ways to deliver an angry letter is to read it aloud to the other person. It's seemingly counterproductive because why would you bother writing everything when you can just say it? However, what you plan to say and what you end up saying are usually very different especially when the unpredictable emotion of anger is concerned. Writing beforehand allows you to collect your thoughts so that you don't leave anything out. What's more, if you tell someone you're about to read a letter they'll most likely wait until you're done before responding. If you're speaking, they'll take liberties with interrupting you and abrasive interruptions always intensify a fight. I recently read a frustrated letter out loud to a friend. She waited until I was finished to react then she took the paper from me and we went over everything point by point. She apologized for some things, I apologized for others, and we agreed to disagree on the rest.

I had an angry letter read to me a few years ago. My boyfriend and

I had gotten into an impassioned argument over the phone. I went to sleep and he started to write. He called me back at 2 A.M. to read what he had written. The letter was long, but it needed to be. Both the letter and the voice he read it in were steady and strong. He wasn't going to waste his time shouting anymore, as he knew I was more likely to respond to the resounding seriousness. Ultimately, we did not survive as a couple, but at the time this letter woke me up—literally and metaphorically.

I don't know where to begin this letter. I don't know how a letter like this should go. As I start, my stomach turns. I really don't want this to be written. I wish this whole situation would just disappear from my awareness. I wish that tonight I could have come home from work, talked about your day, made a few jokes about our wedding party and about your outrageously fat thighs, we could have exchanged "I love you's" and gone to sleep smiling, sighing, with happy hearts in the comfort that another human being several hundred miles away values me in their heart more than anything on earth. For that is how I end most of my nights. But as I sit here I get more upset. I don't have the words. I almost regret not hanging up on you this evening. Leaving you on the other end wondering how deeply you wounded me. Something makes me wish that would have happened because maybe then you might take me seriously. It sickens me to think that I will never have the power over your heart that some immature children who hurt you in the past do. I need to be respected. I need to be cherished the way I cherish you. I need you to feel the same longing in your heart for me. The same feeling that you would do anything in your power to keep me in your life. This is one of those opportunities where you are required to do so. Unfortunately, I can't tell you how, but I want you to recognize the present danger of losing me. I will not go through the rest of my life being treated as a possession that you keep at home, which you know will always be there. I want to be there for you always but I will not if you take my love and adoration for granted. I believe I have never let you down, and I believe I never will. For that is the nature of my love. When I open myself and choose to express love, I do it to my death. I put all other concerns far second to my love. I don't ask anything of you other than to give this thought and appreciate it. Know that I have loved before, not to this dimension, but I have had the blessing of the emotion, and know I am quite capable of it again. I cannot help but feel that there are many people in the world who would pray for a love as pure and honest and complete and unconditional as mine for you. These thoughts are hurting me tremendously to put into words. I keep going back to the dark clouds of your comments tonight. I want to say how dare you gamble with my affection. I want to say how dare you ask me to be like those whom I hate for treating something I hold with such high regard so carelessly. How dare you ask me to treat you with less care and say that you don't feel I have the power to hurt you. It puts strain on my mental well being and on my heart which I am responsible and independent enough to recognize and require your immediate attention. The pain I feel this evening is something that I neither want nor feel I am required to tolerate. I want you to think about your situation. I know because you have told me that no one has ever made such an honest and pure effort to know you. Do you think it will be easy for you to find someone who cares for you as deeply as I do, because I do not. That is no discredit to you, please do not take it that way, because I only wish the whole world saw you as I do. If they did, they would love you forever, just as I do. I do not ask you to change who you are. I would not ask this of anyone.

All I ask is that you evaluate your priorities and either recognize the place where I belong in your heart, a place that seems occupied with a misguided longing for others, or . . . to be honest I don't want to finish the or. I very much want a future together. But I do not, I will not be subject to this kind of emotional strain again. I will not go to sleep restlessly again because of my concern for you, unless you reciprocate my feelings. The outrageous irony of the situation is I can't stop wondering if you're okay. I want to know if you are sleeping soundly or if you are distraught. I know your value upon written words. I know your love for them and your respect and appreciation for them. That, coupled with the fact that it is both therapeutic and necessary for me to write my feelings right now. As I told you, I want this to work out. I want it to work out more than anything in the world. I would do anything in order to make this work, all I ask is that you do the same. I love you.

How to Tell Your Father You're Leaving His House and Never Coming Back

BY EDGAR ALLAN POE (1809-1849)

Daguerreotype of Edgar Allan Poe, taken in November 1948

The father/son relationship between Edgar Allan Poe and John Allan is one of the more tumultuous on record. Edgar's mother, Eliza, a prominent actress, died when she was twenty-four and he was three. His father, David Poe Jr., had left her a year before and was never heard from again. A woman named Frances Allan had sympathized with Eliza during her last days, and after fighting the initial resistance of her husband, she brought the child into their home. As Edgar grew, he became as stubborn and fierce as his foster father, and the two fought frequently. The disastrous dynamic reached its peak in 1827 when Edgar was attending the newly established University of Virginia. Allan did not send much money for the seventeen-year-old student to live off of, so Poe turned to gambling to sustain himself. He returned home in March with a debt of two thousand dollars, and Allan refused to cover any of it. A vicious fight followed that resulted in the following letter. Edgar left and joined the army shortly after. He did eventually resume correspondence with his father when he was hungry for money and affection. The two shared a short-lived reconciliation when Frances Allan died in February 1829. This ended though, when Poe announced he was leaving West Point to become a poet. He tried to visit the only father he knew when he heard Allan was on his deathbed in 1834. Allan reportedly lifted his cane and ordered him out of the room. Edgar was never officially adopted and there was no mention of him in John Allan's will.

MONDAY MARCH 19, 1827
RICHMOND

Sir,

After my treatment on yesterday and what passed between us this morning, I can hardly think you will be surprised at the contents of this letter. My determination is at length taken—to leave your house and indeavor to find some place in this wide world, where I will be treated—not as you have treated me—This is not a hurried determination, but one on which I have long considered—and having so considered my resolution is unalterable—You may perhaps think that I have flown off in a passion, & that I am already wishing to return; But not so—I will give you the reason[s] which have actuated me, and then judge—

Since I have been able to think on any subject, my thoughts have aspired, and they have been taught by you to aspire, to eminence in public life—this cannot be attained without a good Education, such a one I cannot obtain at a Primary school—A collegiate Education therefore was what I most ardently desired, and I had been led to expect that it would at some future time be granted—but in a moment of caprice—you have blasted my hope because forsooth I disagreed with you in an opinion, which opinion I was forced to express—Again, I have heard you say (when you thought I was listening and therefore must have said it in earnest) that you had no affection for me—You have moreover ordered me to quit your house, and are continually upbraiding me with eating the bread of Idleness, when you yourself were the only person to remedy the evil by placing me to some business—You take delight in exposing me before those whom you think likely to advance my interest in the world— You suffer me to be subjected to the whims & caprice, not only of your white family, but the complete authority of the blacks—these grievances I could not submit to; and I am gone. I request that you will send me my trunk containing my clothes & books—if you still have the least affection for me, as the last call I shall make on your bounty, To prevent the fulfillment of the Prediction you this morning expressed, send me as much money as will defray the expenses of my passage to some of the Northern cities & then support me for one month, by which time I shall be enabled to place myself in some situation where I may not only obtain a livelihood, but lay by a sum which one day or another will support me at the University—Send me my trunk &c to the Court-house Tavern, send me I entreat you some money immediately—as I am in the greatest necessity—If you fail to comply with my request—I tremble for the consequence.

Yours &c Edgar A Poe

It depends upon yourself if hereafter you see or hear from me.

3 Return to Sender: Letters that are Hard to Write and Harder to Receive

This time I'm gonna take it myself
and put it right in her hand. And if it comes back
the very next day then I'll understand.

—OTIS BLACKWELL AND WINFIELD SCOTT

It's no glorious task to play the bad guy, but sometimes it's a necessary evil. Feelings never freeze—they live their lives in constant motion, and they update you on what's going on instead of the other way around. An emotional status change can mean many things. Sometimes it means the end of a relationship. Sometimes it means love has invaded a comfortable friendship. It always means things will never be the same.

When it comes time to end a relationship we often find ourselves responsible for the one thing we don't want to be responsible for: Someone else's feelings. The power to hurt another person is a power we might like to have when we're angry, but that's about it. Most other times it's too much of a burden. Oddly, what's on equal par or oftentimes worse than breaking up with someone is telling him or her you have an uncontrollable interest in them when they don't feel the same. Your plan is to flatter and you involuntarily give them reason to avoid you.

Both of these criminal acts make their way to letter form on a regular basis. In a letter the writer is out of harm's way when the message is delivered, and the recipient does not need to conjure up the perfect reaction on the spot. They can think for a while and decide what their response will be, if they respond at all.

BREAKUP LETTERS

I know what the knee-jerk reaction to breakup letters is. It's cowardly. I say not always. Let me ask this, why is love in a letter okay? More than okay—it's considered one of the sweetest gestures of all time. Who says one can't agonize over writing a breakup letter the way they agonize over writing a love letter? It's the same act, different motivation. Also, if a letter helps, honestly helps, the writer to clearly state what they're going through rather than stumble over their words, then that's not a bad thing. As for the recipient, reading a letter gives them a chance to react they way they want. I'm one who often walks away from unpleasant situations thinking of all the things I should have said. A letter gives you time to compose yourself and figure out the best way to handle the situation. For your amusement there is a Web site, sothere.com, which has posted a fresh break-up letter every day for the past six years.

The longer a relationship lasts the more inappropriate ending with a letter seems to be, but the fact of it is that even marriages have ended via letter. In 2003, a book came out entitled *Hell Hath No Fury: Women's Letters from the End of the Affair* (Ballantine, 2002). Editor Anna Holmes compiled more than 100 breakup letters written by women both known and unknown. The oldest one was written around 10 B.C. and the most recent in 2002. The depth of Holmes's collection adds weight to the breakup letter's place in both literature and history. In October 1844, one woman from Philadelphia wrote to her husband, "I did very wrong in marrying you without feeling a sincere attachment." One hundred and fifty-six years later in October 2000, another woman started a letter to her husband with "This is the hardest letter I've ever had to write, and probably the hardest one you'll ever have to read. I'm putting my thoughts and feelings on paper because I want you to hear me out fully before you react."

Naturally, I can't always make a case for breakup letters. They can be plain cowardly. Anyone here care to claim they've never pulled out their coward card? I see no hands raised, mine included. Moving on then.

The breakup letter below is on the angry side—I say that because I think usually they tend to be more on the apologetic, feel-bad side. The good thing about a breakup letter motivated by anger is you don't tiptoe around anything you say. Your point sails majestically across the page, and the other person doesn't wonder what went wrong, they know. On with the story: I dated a man for what felt like the wrong time the whole time. He was just coming out of a relationship and I was out of work and unhappy with myself in general. We agreed we wanted to be in each other's lives, but to what extent meant different things to both of us. He wanted to roll right into an exclusive relationship and I wasn't ready. One of the methods he used to inspire me to see things his way was to go into great detail about his ex-girlfriend and how hard she was working to get him back—a thinly veiled threat. He would also lean into me occasionally and say things like "Now, tell me everything you like about me." I failed that test every time because I was always shocked that he had the audacity to ask such a thing. I felt bad though, because I could tell he wasn't saying it in a haughty way, he just wanted confirmation that our feelings were in the same place and the reality was they weren't. After a few more emotionally trying ordeals on both of our ends this situation never officially ended. It faded away.

Half a year and a much happier time later we got back in touch. We had a pleasant e-mail exchange and agreed to get together. I was excited and had high hopes for it to work out—I blamed the universe for its bad timing and myself for being emotionally unavailable for things not jelling the first time. This time I had just started a new job and successfully put my inner sourpuss back in her cage, and I could tell from his e-mails that he was in a much better place too.

The first five minutes of our reunion was impeccable. It went downhill from there, however. He bought me a drink and said there was someone he wanted me to meet. She was gorgeous. Breathtaking. An Elite model. He made it not so subtly clear that he had been with her during the interim. I sighed and smiled when I realized this was the game we were playing again. Fortunately, I learned at a young age that a beautiful woman is a force you cannot fight, and the wisest course of action is sit back and take in the view. She and I had a great conversation—discussing her work and mine. Now that I'm thinking about it I should have hung out with her, but we moved on. He had some other friends he wanted me to meet.

Before we walked into the second bar, he grabbed my arm and said, "Don't tell them how we met." I guess his past life as a bartender was something he wanted to keep hidden. It was a lovely group of people he introduced me and they were very welcoming. I'm glad they were there because he kept getting up to talk to, yes, another girl. This one was beautiful also, but in an entirely different way. The first one was a blonde bombshell and this one was dark and classic—Ava Gardner-esque. At one point I referred to her as "The Barefoot Contessa" (it was a 1954 movie before it was a Food Network phenomena). He turned to me, raised his left eyebrow, and said, "Jealous?" I should have walked out then, I know. He was an insecure train wreck, and I couldn't turn my eyes away.

Soon after that he pulled me aside, visibly frustrated and said, "We haven't had any time alone." As if they were my friends I insisted we hang out with. We sat at our own table and I decided it was time to tell him about the invisible guy I was dating—this was going to stop before it started again. After that I went home, fell asleep, and woke up infuriated. It usually doesn't happen that way, but my anger took a few hours to soak through. I hated the way he treated me and I hated that I didn't say anything at the time. It wasn't too late. That which had faded away once was now seeing its official end.

The Breakup Letter

From: Samara@emailprovider.com
To: YouHaveGotToBeKiddingMe@emailprovider.com
01/05 (All names in this letter have been changed.)
I apologize in advance for the length and subject matter of this note. I've been seized with the need to be unabashedly honest. I am not seeing anyone. I only said that to put up an immediate barrier between us. Admittedly, it was a coward's call. At first I was excited to see you and hadn't ruled out the possibility of us dating again. But I quickly encountered the same unappealing characteristics that kept me from getting close to you the first time.

The first, and perhaps most unsettling, is your need to put me in direct comparison with other women. Soon after you introduced me to Linda, you smirked and asked if she was rude to me. I'm sure you would have liked it if she had been, knowing that a catfight was taking place in your honor. But no such luck; she was very polite. And again, later that night— calling Melissa The Barefoot Contessa was a reference to her looking like Ave Gardner. Your gut reaction was to initiate the competition and ask if I was jealous. I am a woman who finds myself intrigued and astounded by the beauty of other women—you know this about me. I do not appreciate your trying to transfigure my admiration into jealousy for your own personal gain.

Another trait that has kept me at arm's length is your incessantly asking whether or not I find you attractive. You did this often while we dated and again on Friday night. When I am with someone I'm attracted to, such as yourself, I'm happy to confess that attraction at unpredicted moments. I feel as though I never had a chance to do this with you because you solicit compliments from me on a regular basis by requesting that I tell you all the things I like about you. That's information I prefer to volunteer.

You are a thoughtful person with many redeeming qualities, but your need to be constantly reassured of your looks and talents is off-putting. I hope someday you are comfortable enough in your own skin to know these things are true and have that be enough. I wish you well in all that you do.

Samara

The Response

I didn't know if I should have expected a response to this, and I thought if he did reply he'd rebuke me right back. He wrote the next day, and I hesitantly opened my e-mail. He told me I was right. I didn't believe it either. He didn't say I was right about all of it, but he told me as far as the other women went, it was his inappropriate way of saying "See, other girls like me." I was astonished by his admittance, and he instantly earned back a huge chunk of the respect that he had lost. Our exchange after that ended cordially. We've been in touch sporadically since and wish the best for each other.

Be Specific

Here you try to master the difficult art of being as honest as possible without being cruel. Unless you, like me, are frustrated and fed up. If you're angry the letter will come to you naturally. If you're breaking it off with someone who you don't want to hurt, then the task is unsettling. You should be specific to a certain extent though, because the other person will want to know what went wrong.

✎ *How to Start* If you've been pondering the breakup for a while and know that it's affected your behavior, then consider starting with an explanation: "My attitude lately has been aloof at best and rude at worst. I'm sorry I've waited so long to explain myself." Then go on to explain where you're coming from. Otherwise, you can get to the point and let it be known that this still isn't easy: "I'm not sure where to begin," or "I'm sorry not to do this in person but it's easier for me to put my thoughts on paper."

✐ *When Doing That* Try not to suggest that the problem is fixable. For example, if you say, "This is all my fault, work has been getting to me lately." Work isn't always going to get to you, and they might think once this quarter is over you can give it another go. Imply something more permanent, "I've enjoyed our time together very much, but don't see it going further than it already has."

✐ *Call Yourself a Coward* They're going to call you one anyway, you might as well put it out there that you know what you're doing. Steal my line: "Admittedly, this is a coward's call," or try something like "I'm sure my unwillingness to do this in person disappoints you. It disappoints me too."

✐ *Unless You're Not Being One* If writing the letter is not an act of avoidance but a last resort to get through to someone then make that clear: "I would like to discuss this with you, but you've gotten into the unfortunate habit of not listening to anything I say."

✐ *Disappearing Act* If the letter comes in lieu of one other alternative—walking away without saying anything—then say that. If writing a letter is the act of a chicken, then disappearing with no word is raw poultry on a plate. If they realize that was the only other option, then you may come off as somewhat valiant: "You must know that walking away in silence has been a cloud of temptation over me this entire time—a result of my inadequacies, not yours—but you deserve better than that."

Signing Off

✉ *Ever admiringly & fondly,*   Agnes von Kurowsky (1892–1984), a great love of Ernest Hemingway, ended a very polite yet clear breakup letter this way. Hemingway was crushed. His broken heart went on to inspire both the short story "A Very Short Story," (1925) and the novel *A Farewell to Arms* (1929).

✉ *Never yours,*   In Christine Gallagher's book, *The Woman's Book of Divorce* (Citadel, 2001), a subject named Madeline ends a letter to her ex-husband in this assertive fashion.

✉ *Regretfully,*   Author Rosemarie Keller Skaine used this closing to break up with Bob, her boyfriend in 1954. The letter assures him he has done nothing wrong and there is no one else, she just doesn't have any feelings left for him.

Grammar

Keep it as clean as possible. The other person will take comfort in your mistakes: "You see, he can't even spell!" On second thought, maybe it's kind to give them a few errors to gripe over.

How to Send

You're not going to like what I'm about to say. I think e-mail is best here. If, and I'm saying *if*, you decide you're going to end it via letter, then time is of the essence. You can't mail it because that means you know the relationship has to end on Tuesday and you leave them in the dark until at least Thursday. You can't hand someone a breakup letter because then why wouldn't you just breakup with them in person? E-mail gives the other person an easy and immediate platform to respond if they choose. If you're married or live together then, yes, you can access them easily and put paper in their path (I know it sounds cruel but we've already discussed this). All of the letters in this chapter were sent by e-mail, with the exception of the Sarah Bernhardt letter at the end. She was a brazen woman though; if e-mail had existed in 1847 she would've had no qualms with using it.

How to Break Up with Someone Very Carefully

Although the majority of my Web site customers are women, the occasional man finds his way in. And no, not all of them are looking to write breakup letters, but this gentleman was. He was in perhaps the most difficult breakup situation there is—a change of feelings. This is especially hard because your significant other has done nothing wrong, they walk around being the great person they've always been, but there's some emotional altercation inside you and you'd be untrue to yourself if you kept the relationship going. In a circumstance like this, it's important to accept that the other person will be hurt no matter what, and you can't really throw down a safety net for them. As long as you're honest and respectful, you've done all you can.

(All names in this letter have been changed.)

MARCH 2006

Sarah,

There's no way to say this, but it's impossible not to say it either. I'm sure you've sensed my distance recently, and I owe you an explanation. The trouble is there is no good explanation— any reason I offer will fall short of what you deserve. Before I go any further I want to say that you have done nothing wrong. You are the same angel I started dating earlier this year. What's happened is something has changed within me. I can't identify or fix it, but I know as a result of it I should break up with you. I hate that I just said that. I've been struggling with this, hoping things would click back into place. I fear if we keep moving forward I'll become more and more emotionally detached and I don't want you to have to deal with that. I can try to answer any questions you have. I hope you can forgive me. I truly hope we can be friends. I really mean that.

Justin

Watch the White Lies

White lies are a staple in breakup letters and certainly forgivable to a certain extent. You tell them to protect the other person. Be careful not to white-lie about something you're willing to do though. The breakup letter below was sent to me. It relieved me and then it broke me. It came after days of not hearing from him and knowing something is better than nothing, but knowing this wasn't good.

> **From:** PantsOnFire@emailprovider.com
> **To:** Samara@emailprovider.com
> 12/16/03 10:42 PM
> Hey Samara, What's Up? Sorry for getting back to you so late. Things have been a little weird for me lately. Something/an old someone has come up and we should probably talk about it. It was a bit of a surprise to me. I hate to get you involved and that is why I have strayed away recently. I am a bit of a mental mess at the moment but will try to fix that. I didn't want it to come between us but I guess it sort of has. Anyway I'm working late again tonight so maybe we can get in touch sometime tomorrow or maybe you would rather not talk to me. Either way is understandable.

I zeroed in on six words here, ". . . we should probably talk about it." I knew it would be a hard conversation to have, but at least I could get a few answers and some closure. Oh, if only it were that easy. That part was written just to make the note seem nicer. I know because I called his work phone and his cell phone and his cell phone and his cell phone. Not all in a row—twice that night and twice the next morning. I went to do it again in the early afternoon and realized I was one phone call away from earning my straitjacket stripes. I calmed down and granted myself one final plea over e-mail.

From: Samara@emailprovider.com
To: PantsOnFire@emailprovider.com
12/17/03 1:53 PM

I can respect your decision to reunite with your old girlfriend. Please try to understand though, this is hard for me and I can't just turn off my feelings for you, which is why my desire to speak with you is so strong. Talking to you would help me end this—us—on a good note. But if it's something you don't feel you can do, then I'll respect your stance and hope that some-day we can catch up like old friends. You're a rare find and a truly genuine person. It was a pleasure getting to know you again.

He called me twenty minutes later.

How to Break Up with Someone You Really Like

This is one of those hookup-only situations you treat yourself to every now and then. I had known this guy for years and had always found him attractive. I was told to stay away from him, which made him more at-tractive. It went remarkably well for longer than I had expected, but alas someone was bound to fall and my XX chromosomes insisted that it was me. I promised myself at the beginning though, that in the event of such an ordeal I would back out, no questions asked. To my surprise, I actually did.

From: Samara@emailprovider.com
To: BoyToy@emailprovider.com
04/12/06 09:55 AM

Hey, what's up—I realize this is going to catch you off guard and I apologize for that. I've been thinking now might be a good time to end this. It's not for a bad reason at all but rather a good one in that I can sense my interest in you head-ing in a new direction. I realize though, this was never meant to be that, and I think it might be best to pull out before things get complicated. We're always going to travel in the same social circle and run into each other on many occasions and I don't want to risk it ever being awkward. I enjoy your company (amongst other things) and look forward to a continued friendship.

I hope this doesn't seem cold or formal over e-mail. I know in most cases such things should take place over the phone or in person, but in our case I think that might make it more uncomfortable. We can talk though, if you like—I just wanted to get it all out here first. Please don't be weirded out—just be flattered. You're attractive, successful, fun, and all those other cli-chéd things women tend to like in men ;)

The Aftermath

Sometimes you send a breakup message and know that you may never hear back. This was not one of those. I honestly expected a reply—not a complicated one, just a quick acknowledgment of what I had said and an acceptance of my friendship. A little more than twenty-four hours later, I was frustrated when I hadn't heard anything. More amusing than any response he could have sent though, is me hashing the situation out with my friend Elise. WARNING: You are about to witness the breakdown of inexplicable male behavior by two overanalytical, occasionally conniving members of the female gender.

From: Elise@emailprovider.com
To: Samara@emailprovider.com
4/13/06 02:08 PM
Whoa, this is really honest . . . in a good way. It sounds totally casual and nice, and just simple. It sounds like you like him but not in a scary way. I'm rather shocked he hasn't replied. If he doesn't reply, he's truly a dick. And he's the one who will make it awkward. I can't imagine why he wouldn't reply to

this. You're making things really easy for him. How do you feel about it?

From: Samara@emailprovider.com
To: Elise@emailprovider.com
4/13/06 02:09 PM
I'm happy with it. I think it's all those things you said, and his response wouldn't have to be deep. It could be "Thanks for this. I appreciate your understanding that I don't want to be in anything that resembles a relationship right now, but I would like to stay friends."

From: Elise@emailprovider.com
To: Samara@emailprovider.com
4/13/06 02:14 PM
That's the thing . . . ANYTHING. An acknowledgement. "Thanks for your honesty." "Sounds good." Even a "Thanks for this. We're on the same page." I hope for his sake that he's home sick or something. But even if it's awkward, which it totally will be now, YOU shouldn't feel awkward. I mean, if you do, you should feel awkward FOR him.

From: Samara@emailprovider.com
To: Elise@emailprovider.com
4/13/06 02:21 PM
Correct me if I'm wrong, but I do believe at the stroke of midnight tonight this automatically becomes fodder for the book?

From: Elise@emailprovider.com
To: Samara@emailprovider.com
4/13/06 02:24 PM
Midnight is being generous. Perhaps a chapter entitled: "Even when you try to be mature and let guys off the hook, they act like pussies anyway." Do you like it?

From: Samara@emailprovider.com
To: Elise@emailprovider.com
4/13/06 02:27 PM
Brilliant! It will be followed up with a subhead section: "What he could have/should have written to me". And I will include all of your very simple, one-sentence suggestions. Let the record show that he is the only man who may appear in the book who knew the entire time that I had been commissioned to write aforementioned book at the time of official blow-off.

From: Elise@emailprovider.com
To: Samara@emailprovider.com
4/13/06 02:44 PM
If he wanted to be in the book why didn't he just say so? Since he knew you were writing a book about LETTER WRITING, and still didn't reply, then all's fair in love and book publishing.

Now, to his credit he did eventually write me the short response I had hoped for. He sent it on April 18 at 9:40 A.M.—six days later. I had given up on hearing from him after the third. He sent four sentences saying that he respected where I was coming from, etc. The length of the e-mail didn't bother me at all, but the time did: five days/four sentences. That's an invalid equation enabling me to give him a hard time. Plus, by that point he was already 105 hours and 40 minutes past the keep-him-out-of-the-book deadline.

How to Tell a Man You No Longer Love Him

BY SARAH BERNHARDT (1844-1923)

Sixteen-year-old Sarah Bernhardt, portrait by Nadar

Paris-born actress Sarah Bernhardt was a sensation on the stage and had an equally absorbing love life. She worked as a courtesan before her acting career took her all over Europe in the 1870s. Her long list of lovers includes the Belgian Prince de Ligne, novelist Jean Richepin, artist Gustave Doré, and countless actors. One of those actors was Jean Mounet-Sully (1841–1916) whom she met in 1872. "The Divine Sarah," as she came to be known, made the first move, inviting him to meet her that same night. The two had a tumultuous affair, which was strained by Sarah's refusal to commit. When it finally ended, Jean had trouble accepting her position and continued to ask where their relationship was going. She wrote this letter to clear things up.

JANUARY *1874*

As far as I know I have done nothing to justify such behavior, I've told you distinctly that I do not love you any longer. I shook your hand and asked you to accept friendship in place of love. Why do you reproach me? Surely not for a lack of frankness. I have been loyal: I have never deceived you; I have been yours completely. It's your fault that you have not known how to hold on to what is yours.

Besides, dear Jean, you must realize that I am not made for happiness. It is not my fault that I am constantly in search of new sensations, new emotions. That is how I shall be until my life is worn away. I am just as unsatisfied in the morning after, as I am the night before. My heart demands more excitement than anyone can give it. My frail body is exhausted by the act of love. Never is it the love I dream of.

At this moment I am in a complete prostration. My life seems to have stopped. I feel neither joy nor sorrow. I wish you could forget me. What can I do? You must not be angry with me. I'm an incomplete person but a good one at heart. If I could prevent your suffering I would do so!!! But you demand my love and it is you who have killed it!

I beg you, Jean, let us be friends.

UNAUTHORIZED LOVE LETTERS

It's remarkable how little control we have over our emotions. The brain that causes you to say to yourself, "No, you can't think this way," or "You must feel that way," is the same brain that deliberately disobeys and insists you suffer in the process. This is especially true with the drug of an emotion we call love. Hence the expression "falling in love." We don't call it "casually strolling into love" or "making an appointment with love," because basically you trip, you fall, and you are now facedown in the mud, trying to get your bearings. It's great if the other person is rolling around in the mud with you, but few things are messier then being stuck there by yourself in unrequited chaos.

In *The Book of Love: Writers and Their Love Letters* (Plume/Penguin, 1992), author Cathy N. Davidson writes: "Writing such letters, we often come to appreciate our own complexities and understand that the real purpose of writing letters is to fall a little bit in love with our self. In this process, the actual beloved is just an innocent bystander." I find this especially true of writing to someone you've fallen for who hasn't fallen for you. It's a very selfish thing to do. Your feelings have spiraled out of control and, by confessing, you're insisting the other person deal with them too. Your assertion of love is unauthorized. That being said, I do think selfishness in moderation is necessary. After all you're not much good to other people if you can't look out for yourself, so writing unauthorized love letters is like any other seemingly insurmountable challenge—you never know unless you try. Except sometimes you do know and you still have to try.

I wrote the following letter when it was authorized, or when I *thought* it was authorized. I was dating a man I adored and by all appearances he was right there with me. He never kept me waiting, called on cue, and was rehearsed and ready at all times to perform some gentlemanly gesture, give an uncanny compliment, or flatter me silently with a gripping stare. Admittedly, I fell at lightning speed. There was no reason not to. As Christmas came closer I wanted to write him something as amazing as I thought he was.

I'm sure you've guessed where this is going—straight down. Shortly after I wrote the letter but before I gave it to him, he started backing away slowly, as if he could smell my serenity. The calls came less frequently. The e-mails missed their romantic mark and soon stopped altogether. I immediately went into a senseless scramble to try and figure out what went wrong and fix it fast. Finally, after almost a week of not hearing from him—as you all know that's the equivalent of three long lifetimes when you've got it bad—I received an e-mail from him (see The Breakup Letter on page 62) telling me he was getting back together with his ex-girlfriend. Against my will it ended, and I was stuck with my stupid feelings and my stupid letter that went undelivered.

When all was said and done the one thing that mystified me most was that I hadn't heard of this girlfriend. He and I were very open when it came to stories, both good and bad, about our exes. So the fact that I knew nothing of her, when she was clearly still in his life, baffled me. I was to find out soon enough that the reason I hadn't heard of her was because she was not his ex-girlfriend, bur rather his full-time, "exclusive" girlfriend the entire time. I imagine I was one final fling before they moved in together. On second thought, I probably shouldn't fool myself into thinking I was his final fling. The way I found all this out: He told me. He didn't realize it, but he did.

The way the story goes is that I took my exit and stayed away for a little more than two months. I dated someone almost immediately to aid in the get-over-it process—that's actually not a good idea. Against all laws of logic, my feelings stayed steadfast and strong. One day I reread the letter I had written him and could still support every word with my full body weight. For whatever it was worth I wanted him to have it. There was no one else on the planet Earth I could give it to.

I e-mailed asking what he'd been up to—trying to veil my intentions behind the disguise of friendship. Seeing straight through that, he wrote back and suggested we get together, which I was hoping he'd do. It came as no surprise to me that we had a great time. Conversation came easily to us, as did laughter and passion. When his relationship situation came up, he said that, just as things hadn't worked out so many times before with this girlfriend, they weren't working out again. I believed him because I wanted to. He also told me a lot more about how this relationship came to be and why it wasn't going anywhere— that'll be important in a minute.

As planned, the evening ended with me giving him the letter. I told him I had written it before and still wanted him to have it. The one thing that I didn't do, or consider doing, was change the letter. It was still written as if everything had worked out, which I knew could be daunting, but it was too honest in its original form for me to tamper with. I knew the response would be one of two extremes. There's the Hollywood version: He reads the letter in the car, walks back up to my door, and we consummate the fact that we feel the same way with unbridled ferocity. Then there's the independent film version: I watch him drive away, know I'll never hear from him again, and figure out later what had gone on through a series of fluorescent flashbacks. This chapter has already lent itself to the latter.

In the days that followed, the imminent overanalyzation took place and I rethought everything he had told me about his girlfriend. Circles didn't fit into squares. This was different than the story I had originally been given. I mentally replayed our first round, inserted these new findings, and saw what had gone on. In him telling me why it wouldn't work out, I realized that that he already knew it would. Finding out it had to end was upsetting. Finding out it was never real to begin with, even more so. It hurt the hell out of me.

One might think discovering this would make for instant regret and a longing to retract the letter, but no. I just existed temporarily in that paradoxical purgatory where nothing, not even the reality of another person's actions, can turn your feelings off. Part of me held out hope that the man I handed the letter to might someday give it to the man I wrote it for. If it could make that man smile on a rainy day then yes, it was worth it.

The Unauthorized Love Letter

DECEMBER 2003

Dear R——

I hope this finds you happy and ready to end the year on a good note. This year for me was clarifying—I learned a lot about myself as I was forced to rely on my own survival skills and was reminded of the importance of exercising optimism when things don't go my way. But to my unexpected pleasure the one thing that did go my way this year was you. You were just a pleasant memory of mine and somehow materialized and became an authentic and very intense presence. The opportunities to get to know you and wake up tangled in your warm body were pleasantries I had once hoped for but never truly anticipated. I'm so grateful that you allowed me access to you, and I thought it only fair that you know why I'm so drawn to you. In all honesty, this letter is really a pathetic attempt on my part to project myself into your mind the way you inadvertently projected yourself into mine. The following is a list of some of your charming qualities—according to me.

I'm sure there's a thousand more and I hope in time you'll reveal them to me also. For now, these will have to do:

—First, I'm drawn to your steadfast ambitions—the ones that keep you in constant motion, aching to improve upon your already impressive accomplishments.

—Then there's your modesty—you're always content to reject the well-deserved compliments I give you regarding how clever and attractive you are.

—Next, there's your broad taste in music.

—I'm moved by your concern for your siblings—taking it upon yourself to correct the mistakes your parents have made.

—And how could I not mention your brilliant body with every sinew and muscle exercised perfectly into place.

—I like your bottom lip—so good for biting.

—I'm grateful for the compliments you pay me at the most unexpected moments.

—I'm a big fan of your right shoulder blade.

—Okay, I like the left one too.

—I appreciate how polite you are and how often you say thank you.

—I love that you're always you—whether we're with your friends, my friends, or if it's just us.

—I love when it's just us.

—And then there's the way you kiss me.

—Then there's the way you make me ache.

—Then there's the way you taste.

—Then there's the way you feel.

—Then there's the way you make me feel.

—Then there's how tender you are.

—Then there's how aggressive you are.

—And finally there's your beautiful face—that mixes perfectly the novelties, expressions, and wonder of a boy with all the temptations and certainties of a man. In case you haven't noticed, I'm quite taken with you. I wish you well this year and always.

With adoration, Samara

Be Specific

This is love you're willing to humiliate yourself for—be more than specific, be shameless. As English logician and philosopher Bertrand Russell once said, "Of all forms of caution, caution in love is perhaps the most fatal to true happiness."

The consensus among my girlfriends was that the letter I wrote was nice but way too heavy. A woman would be able to handle something like this but not a man. Ladies, I love you but I'm going to go ahead and officially disagree. I'm sorry, men can't handle what? Being told how great they are? No, I'm sure they're well equipped to handle that, and I think women's assumptions that they don't need to hear it as often is unfortunate. However, they are only equipped to hear it from women they want to hear it from. The only problem with this letter is the writer. It was me he didn't like, not the letter. But I know if I had written a lighter version with the hopes of keeping him around a little longer, the same thing would have happened. Except I would have thought to myself: *If that was my only chance to tell him how I felt, then why didn't I tell him how felt?*

> *How to Start* I realize my circumstance was special and you may be writing your letter to someone, a friend perhaps, with whom you've never been romantic. In that case, or even the case of falling for a casual acquaintance, open in a simple, friendly way: "I hope you're doing well," or "It was great to see you last night." Follow up with a quick transition sentence such as, "I haven't been able to stop thinking about you and decided I would let you in on how I feel." Then, let your love loose.

> *Friendship Folly* Be honest with yourself about the reality of friendship after the letter. If you can't bear to be around the person once you know they know how you feel, then it's best to be clear about that: "I never expected to feel this way and certainly didn't plan on disrupting our friendship, but I'm afraid it's gone that far." If you think friendship is still viable: "I realize it may take a while for us to recover from my sudden admission, but our friendship is indescribably important to me and I want to make sure we hold on to it."

> *Make Up Your Mind* Unauthorized love letters can be delivered in the midst of a relationship too. This could come about in the event that you want to move forward and the other person is content standing still. If you've reached your breaking point and it's time to come up with an articulate way of saying, "Shit or get off the pot!" Then try something like:

"This is not an ultimatum, it's an invitation. I love you and am inviting you into my life full-time."

🖋 *Against the Odds* Just so you know, the house almost always wins here. I've never known of an unauthorized love letter that actually accomplished its designated task. As I said earlier, this is something you do for you. Why? I share with you the content of a sign I once saw in a greeting card store: "Twenty years from now you'll regret the things you didn't do more than you'll regret the things you did."

Signing Off

Unauthorized love letters can end the same way regular love letters do. You've already put it out there that you've fallen for them, so why not end it with a bang?

✉ *Farewell—farewell—come to me if you love me,* From George Foster to Rufus Wilmot Griswold, a glorious and very dangerous way to end an unauthorized love letter (you'll read about these two in just a moment under Man-to-Man).

Grammar

You can't be as careless here as you would with an authorized love letter. Keep in mind (as if you could forget) this person is not enamored with you and won't read it with the same rose-colored glasses that an established lover would. Chances are though, this person is in love with him- or herself, so if you say enough nice things they'll surely overlook a few grammatical flaws.

How to Send

Sign it. Seal it. Deliver it. You need the other person's undivided attention here and just the act of opening an envelope or unfolding a piece of paper can remove someone from their world for a moment. Since this is not something they're expecting, seeing it squished between dozens of e-mails could cause it to be overlooked or read in a rush.

If You Receive An Unauthorized Love Letter

Maybe it's just me, but I think it's nice to respond to these. Not easy, but nice. Let me remind you that the one thing the sender wants to know, above all else, is that you received the letter. Once they know that, then they know everything. Your response doesn't have to be as detailed or intimate as theirs. Your responding is a sign of respect for their feelings, and they're less likely to harbor hope of being with you someday if you're up front with them. Otherwise they may think no news is good news. Silence tends to breed hope. If you're stuck, these should help:

- *If you're single* "Wow, I don't know what to say. I think thank you is at the top of my list. Your letter was beyond flattering. I am undeserving of it, which makes it especially hard for me to tell you that I don't share your affection. It would be incredibly inconsiderate for me to lead you to believe otherwise."

- *If you're in a relationship* "I'll admit I'm embarrassed by all the kindnesses you wrote to me. It took a lot of courage for you to say those things and I want you to know I recognize that. The fact is though, I am very much in love with my girlfriend [boyfriend/husband/wife]. I am certain you will share an extraordinary love with someone someday."

One-shot Deal

Here's the rule: You can send an unauthorized love letter one time only. Let me assure you, you will be tempted to send two, three, or twenty. You'll be astonished at your own ability to convince yourself that they couldn't possibly have received the letter. If they had gotten the letter, then they'd be in your arms right now, right? A pack of evil trolls must have intercepted it or, even worse, malicious dragons attacked the mailman. Poor mailman. Some cyberspace magician must be rerouting all the e-mails. There is no other explanation! Unfortunately, the only explanation here is the one you don't want to hear. In my case you have to say to yourself firmly, but not cruelly and preferably out loud, "Samara, sweetheart, you handed it to him."

I advocate these letters because you are entitled to your feelings; however, the other person is also entitled to theirs. If their feelings are not in your favor, you must reverence that. When I was in high school, a good guy friend of mine started receiving love confessions from a fellow classmate of ours. This girl was extremely shy. I was shocked that she had it in her to write the notes, but she wrote them. She wrote them on paper, on napkins, on anything she could find. She would creep up behind him, stick one in his hand, and walk away, saying nothing. It got to the point where he wanted a restraining order. If I were to point this girl out to you in a crowd and tell you someone wanted a restraining order against her, you'd laugh out loud. Regardless, her incessant writing and refusal to take no for an answer terrified him. He didn't end up getting the restraining order—I think he said something to her mother. Needless to say, they never came close to dating.

Reread and Reconcile

One of my favorite things about letters is they can be experienced and re-experienced. The thoughts of one moment are preserved and you can encounter them again as an older, hopefully wiser version of yourself. Case in point, the following letter. I went to a small high school and thought I knew everyone, so it surprised me when I made a new friend my senior year. He and I met working together after school, so there was ample opportunity to get to know each other. I suspected he was interested in me, but dismissed it readily as I didn't want him to be. I was happy being his friend. He then took a bold step forward and wrote this in my yearbook:

Hi Samara,

I can't believe we never met before this year, but I'm glad we finally did! I've grown to love you as a friend and hate to see you run off to college. You are one of the most interesting people I've met and I'll always cherish the times we've had together (Charlie Brown). I'm glad I'm leaving work because I can't stand it without you. I guess what I'm trying to say is, I love you! There's no way around it. You can't run now that you've read it you must accept it. Thank you for being so tolerant of me all this time and keep in touch.

Love, *Randy*

After I read this I took it upon myself to e-mail him and explain that he had gotten it all wrong. He actually didn't love me. He didn't know me that well and couldn't possibly love me. We continued to spend time together platonically through the summer, but I was condescending on several occasions as I felt the need to cure him of his interest in me.

Years later I was flipping though my yearbook and came across his remarkably thoughtful and courageous message. I also (unfortunately) remembered my reaction to it. Will you pardon me for a moment while I berate my seventeen-year-old self: You inconsiderate little brat! Who the hell do you think you are, telling someone how they do or do not feel? You told him he wasn't in love with you because thinking that way made *you* feel better. It's not always about you. Learn this now and your love and life will be a lot easier. You can certainly show more respect for him and his feelings than that.

Randy, will you please accept the long overdue apology of a tactless teenager, the victim of her own insecurities no doubt, who has since dismounted her high horse? And thank you. Thank you so much.

Man-to-Man

I include this simply because it's one of the most beautiful unrequited love sentiments I've ever encountered, and I had to dust it off. It was written to a man named Rufus Wilmot Griswold (1815–1857). In his lifetime, Griswold was the editor of several poetry anthologies—the most famous being *Poets and Poetry of America* (1842)—as well as being the well-known nemesis of Edgar Allan Poe. Several years before Griswold walked among the literary elite, he was living in Albany, New York (circa 1835), with a twenty-year-old journalist named George G. Foster (d. 1856). After three years together, Griswold, famous for random acts of departure, grew antsy and left Albany. Foster wrote and pleaded for his return.

> I have loved often and deeply. My heart has burned itself almost to a charred cinder by the flames of passion which have glowed within it—and yet I have never felt toward any human being—man or woman—so strong and absorbing an affection as I bear to you.

Foster closed with, "Farewell—farewell—come to me if you love me." The two men never got back together, but Griswold held on to the letter for the rest of his life.

How to Write to Your Immortal Beloved

BY LUDWIG VAN BEETHOVEN (1770-1827)

Illustration of Beethoven by Carl Jager

Marked by a smashing professional life and tragic personal life, German composer Ludwig van Beethoven still stands today as one of the principal players in classical music. He moved to Vienna in his early twenties and settled into his craft by writing several notable pieces. His life took a drastic turn around the age of twenty-eight, when he started going deaf. He contemplated suicide several times as his condition worsened. Ultimately though, he accepted the irrevocable physical challenge and continued to compose masterful, passionate music.

Beethoven never married. He had a penchant for women who were married or unattainable in some other way. Around 1812, he fell madly in love with a enigmatic woman who we know today only as Immortal Beloved. He wrote her a trilogy of letters over two days while staying at a Czech spa in Teplitz—he had gone there to recover from failing health. These unalloyed letters were not only unauthorized but also undelivered as they were found among his possessions after his death. They were not unauthorized in the sense that she did not reciprocate his love, by the way he writes it appears as though she did, but in that their situation was impossible and they didn't end up together. There have been many guesses as to who this mysterious muse was—no absolute conclusions have been made. One strong contender is a married woman he met in Vienna in 1810 named Antonie Brentano.

JULY 6, 1812, IN THE MORNING

My angel, my all, my very self—Only a few words today and at that with pencil (with yours)—Not till tomorrow will my lodgings be definitely determined upon—what a useless waste of time—Why this deep sorrow when necessity speaks—can our love endure except through sacrifices, through not demanding everything from one another; can you change the fact that you are not wholly mine, I not wholly thine—Oh God, look out into the beauties of nature and comfort your heart with that which must be—Love demands everything and that very justly—thus it is to me with you, and to you with me. But you forget so easily that I must live for me and for you; if we were wholly united you would feel the pain of it as little as I—My journey was a fearful one; I did not reach here until four o'clock yesterday morning. Lacking horses the post-coach chose another route, but what an awful one; at the stage before the last I was warned not to travel at night; I was made fearful of a forest, but that only made me the more eager—and I was wrong. The coach must needs break down on the wretched road, a bottomless mud road. Without such postilions as I had with me I should have remained stuck in the road. Esterhazy, traveling the usual road here, had the same fate with eight horses that I had with four—Yet I got some pleasure out of it, as I always do when I successfully overcome difficulties—Now a quick change to things internal from things external. We shall surely see each other soon; moreover, today I cannot share with you the thoughts I have had during these last few days touching my own life—If our hearts were always close together, I would have none of these. My heart is full of so many things to say to you—ah—there are moments when I feel that speech amounts to nothing at all—Cheer up—remain my true, my only treasure, my all as I am yours. The gods must send us the rest, what for us must and shall be—Your faithful Ludwig

EVENING, MONDAY, JULY 6

You are suffering, my dearest creature—only now have I learned that letters must be posted very early in the morning on Mondays to Thursdays—the only days on which the mail-coach goes from here to K.—You are suffering—Ah, wherever I am, there you are also—I will arrange it with you and me that I can live with you. What a life!!! Thus!!! Without you—pursued by the goodness of mankind hither and thither—which I as little want to deserve as I deserve it——Humility of man towards man——it pains me——and when I consider myself in relation to the universe, what am I and what is He——whom we call the greatest——and yet——herein lies the divine in man——I weep when I reflect that you will probably not receive the first report from me until Saturday——Much as you love me——I love you more——But do not ever conceal yourself from me——good night——As I am taking the baths I must go to bed—— Oh God——so near! So far! Is not our love truly a heavenly structure, and also as firm as the vault of Heaven?

GOOD MORNING, ON JULY 7

Though still in bed, my thoughts go out to you, my Immortal Beloved, now and then joyfully, then sadly, waiting to learn whether or not fate will hear us——I can live only wholly with you or not at all——Yes, I am resolved to wander so long away from you until I can fly to your arms and say that I am really at home with you, and can send my soul enwrapped in you into the land of spirits——Yes, unhappily it must be so——You will be the more contained since you know my fidelity to you. No one else can ever possess my heart——never—— never——Oh God, why must one be parted from one whom one so loves. And yet my life in V is now a wretched life——Your love makes me at once the happiest and the unhappiest of men——At my age I need a steady, quiet life——can that be so in our connection? My angel, I have just been told that the mail-coach goes every day——therefore I must close at once so that you may receive the letter at once——Be calm, only by a clam consideration of our existence can we achieve our purpose to live together——Be calm——love me——today——yesterday—— what tearful longings for you——you——you——my life——my all——farewell. Oh continue to love me——never misjudge the most faithful heart of your beloved.

ever thine

ever mine

ever ours

4   Letters of Gratitude

What language shall I borrow to thank thee, dearest friend?
—PAUL GERHARDT

Few emotional glories compare with unscheduled moments of unabashed gratefulness—those sweet seconds you come to realize that someone you know well or barely know at all has done something incredibly thoughtful, helpful, remarkably unselfish and you are the beneficiary, whether you deserve it or not. It could be the gift they gave or the fact that they drove all night to deliver it. It could be the umbrella they held over your head or that they watched the kids while you had to run out quickly. It could be the kind words they offered before you walked on-stage or the hug they gave you afterwards. Whatever it was, it momentarily improved your life and they asked for nothing in return.

I liken gratefulness to helplessness. For a moment you are helpless in the face of someone else's kindness and you don't have the words to explain how much their actions really mean. It's good to be helpless sometimes. It serves as a gentle reminder that we really can't get by without each other. Truth be told, my favorite moments of gratitude are the ones that will never make their way to paper—those exchanged between strangers on the street. Naturally, when you know someone well enough to write and embellish your thank-you, you should do so as soon as possible.

THANK-YOU LETTERS

I nominate "thank you" to be recognized as the second most important phrase in the English language (you nominate the first). Let there be no fear of overusing this phrase, and let there be no limits as to whom you extend it to. Let there also be no limits concerning thank-you letters— no limits to the occasions for which you write them and no maximum number of times you write them. Don't restrict yourself to only writing thank-you notes after receiving expected gifts—birthdays, weddings, holidays, etc.—but also after receiving unexpected gifts—impromptu car rides home, solid pieces of advice, help moving into your new apartment. And remember, an excuse to write someone and thank them doesn't have to be reserved for any particular event or service—you can always thank someone for just being them. Gratitude is contagious, may it infect us all.

Believe it or not, this chapter is more personal to me than any of the others. These letters feel so strange to show, because all I have in the way of thank-you notes are the ones that have been written to me. The ones I write are written by hand and given away for good. The people who've written here have been more than generous and this feels like the "See How Great Samara Is" chapter. I assure you, this is not my intention, and encourage you to think much more highly of these featured writers.

To start, I leave you in the hands of my very good friend Lori. We've been friends since freshman year of college, and no one in my life has been more consistent with sending gratitude-inspired correspondence. Each time we spend a weekend together it's followed up with a thank-you card, and several times a year I receive an unsolicited "just thinking about you" or "something reminded me of you" card. They arrive, always written by hand and usually with a much-appreciated inspirational saying on the front. This has not changed in ten years—what has changed is my gifts to her have gotten better.

The Thank-you Letters

AUGUST 1999

My dearest Samara—

What a pleasure it was for you to grace my twenty-first party! I hope your trip to see Daniel one last time was safe and exciting. Thank you for the Swedish Fish and the makeup case. I love the box. So far I've used the "fashion" lipstick and I love the way it shimmers. Thanks again. Good luck this semester with grades, boys, and the paper. Keep in touch.

Love, *Lori*

Be Specific

Be short and specific. Thank-you notes need not be long and complicated, just enthusiastic. They can follow this basic formula: Mention the place, the gift, and the next time.

- *The Place* Start off with saying how great it was to see them at whatever place: "Thank you for meeting me for lunch." "I'm so glad you came to my party." "Thank you for sharing my wedding day with me." If there was no meeting place, then mention the missed one: "I'm sorry you weren't able to make your way out here this year. You were missed very much! Your thoughtful bouquet of flowers arrived safe and sound and continues to brighten up the living room."

- *The Exception* Some gifts arrive like clockwork every year from relatives we never see. In this case, start with the other person's well being then focus on the gift: "Aunt Susan, I hope

> Dear Samara — 8/28/05
> I had a *wonderful* time
> with you at the beach.
> I was _so_ relaxed. Thank
> you so much for the gift
> to parasail. It was
> amazing! It definitely
> goes down in the books!
> Have a wonderful month
> of September ... 26 is
> an awesome year ... you'll
> love it! Good luck with
> the Philly house search ...
> of course I want you
> closer to me! Take care!
>   Love,
>   Lori

you had a wonderful year and that Trixie has stopped scratch-ing up your curtains."

🕉 ***The Gift, If You Liked It*** Then your job is easy. Mention the gift and how you've used it. "Thank you for the gorgeous sweater—I've worn it three times already." "Thank you for the Apple gift certificate—I've added fifty great songs to my iPod."

🕉 ***The Gift, If You Didn't Like It*** You don't have to go on and on, just mention it once and then center your excitement around the giver instead: "Thank you for the Sigmund Freud action figure, and especially thank you for coming to the barbecue.

It was a pleasure to catch up and to hear all about your trip to Greece—your tan looks fabulous."

🖎 *Next Time*   End with a nod toward the next time you'll see each other. "I look forward to seeing you as soon as school starts." "Let's make plans again soon." "Please, make sure to stop by the next time you're in town." If it's a person you know you won't see anytime soon you can allude to the next phone call or the next holiday/occasion you'll be in touch.

🖎 *Thank You for the Random Act of Kindness*   These types of thank-you notes don't follow any rules, but it's hard to go wrong with them as they're rarely expected. "Thank you for listening to me last night. I was in terrible shape and you were kind to lend your ear." "Thank you for helping me change my tire in the pouring rain. I don't know what I would have done without you."

Signing Off

✉ *With deep gratitude and all my best wishes,*   Written in November 1998—a thank-you letter from famed *Cosmopolitan* editor, Helen Gurley Brown, to the surgeon that performed her breast cancer surgery.

✉ *I shall always be infinitely grateful to you.*   From savvy Sarah Bernhardt to Jean Mounet-Sully (the same man whose heart she broke on page 67). In November of that same year (1874) they came to an understanding and she wrote a short letter thanking him for forgiving her and ending in this way.

✉ *Affectionately, Devotedly, Lovingly, Faithfully yours,*   As per Emily Post (featured at the end of this chapter).

✉ *Gratefully, Thankfully, Appreciatively,*   Other options along the same lines.

✉ *Best wishes, All best, All my best, Best,*   The "best" ways to end.

Grammar

As you'll see in a moment, my recommendation for sending thank-you notes is to handwrite them. Grammar is more easily overlooked in handwritten notes, as handwriting takes longer for the eyes to navigate through than type. Not to mention the recipient may find it foreign to receive a handwritten note and the gesture alone will distract them. Just try to get the basics right—spelling, periods, capitals, and commas. Admittedly, I'm a horrible speller and will sometimes type thank-you notes out to make sure everything is spelled correctly before I copy it down.

How to Send

Always. Yes, always. One more time: Always write these by hand. In writing by hand, you immediately humble yourself, and from this un-assuming position you can offer your most sincere thanks. Then hand them over or mail them—thank you letters alone should keep the U.S. postal service up and running.

I received a preprinted thank-you note for a wedding gift once. The stationery was pretty as was the script, but it was cold, especially in knowing that everyone else had received the same generic message. I know it's daunting when you have a large group of thank-you letters to write, but it's still important that each person receive their own individual message. If they were worthy of an invite, they are worthy of a thank-you. If you had 1,000 guests attend your wedding, then the first administrative task you should perform as a married couple is to sit down and write 500 thank-you cards each—of course, make it fun and take sex breaks after every 100. Okay fine, fifty.

If You Receive a Thank-you Letter

Enjoy. There's no need to thank for the thank-you, as the original gift was your act of kindness. If you were especially moved by the note you can send a quick e-mail letting the other person know you received it and appreciate it.

Thank You for the Thank-You

Of course rules were made to be broken, and if you want to hand-write someone a thank-you for the thank-you then all you risk is ending up in a cycle of complimentary correspondence. There are worse things.

This thank-you for the thank-you note is from an extraordinary woman: The Reverend Anne Richards. We walked in each other's way for three years, as she was one of the presiding priests at the church I attend. Her kindness is a constant presence and her insights shrewd. It was her unshakable voice that lent comfort to me and the other emotionally exhausted congregants gathered on the National Day of Prayer following September 11—we assembled two miles from Ground Zero. When the time came for her to move on, I wrote her a thank-you-for-all-you've-done letter and she replied courteously:

ANNE RICHARDS

March 16, 2004

Dear Samara,

Many thanks for your card and kind words of farewell. It has been a complete pleasure and joy to get to know you a bit at Grace! Thank you for all you do to upbuild the community there. Your presence and participation are so gracious and competent! Keep on keepin' on sister!

Love and blessings,
Anne ✝

Split-Second Letters

I just came up with the name for this subversion of thank-you letters—I hope you like it. We, as human beings, move in and out of each other's lives all the time, and there are many wonderful people who we know for only a short while—in the grand scheme of things, about a split second. It could be a teacher, fellow student, boss, or acquaintance of some sort, and you've come to admire their work ethic, sense of humor, or you just ended up sharing coffee with them several times and enjoyed their company. Although your friendship may not go the distance and you won't necessarily keep in touch, a note thanking them for the temporary role they played in your life is thoughtful and will be remembered. I recommend these especially when leaving a job. Thanking a boss who played the role of mentor or a fellow coworker for their guidance and wishing them well will keep you in each other's good graces for a long time, and this can come back to help you.

The unexpected and very considerate note below is from a sorority sister of mine. Yes, I was in a sorority (simmer down back there). Despite the bad rap they get, I'd list it as one of the more positive experiences of my life—especially my senior year when I was president. Sorority girls, the ones I knew anyway, are very good at sending each other notes of encouragement. This came from one sister I didn't know that well. She and I got along but hadn't spent much time together outside the group. She wrote this following at a retreat everyone had gone on but that I was unable to attend:

> Samara,
>
> I just wanted to write a quick note to let you know how much you are appreciated! You put forth much more time and effort than most of us realize. I don't want you to ever think that the things you do for our sorority go unnoticed. I give you all the credit in the world for taking on such a huge responsibility~ and not only did you take it on, you mastered it! :) We missed your "sunshine" at the retreat!

How to Express Your Utmost Gratitude in Ways You Never Thought of

—BY EMILY POST (1873–1960)

Illustration by James Montgomery Flagg

For more than eighty years, the name Emily Post has been synonymous with etiquette, as she literally wrote the book on it. She was born Emily Price in October 1873 in Baltimore, Maryland. She was educated privately and traveled extensively. In 1892, she married a banker named Edwin Post. They later divorced and she wrote whimsical novels about European and American society to help support her two young sons, Edwin and Bruce. In 1922, she wrote *Etiquette in Society, in Business, in Politics, and at Home* (later retitled *Etiquette: The Blue Book of Social Use*) and it was a runaway hit—going through ten editions in her lifetime. She went on to host a radio program and write a syndicated newspaper column.

One might expect the mother of etiquette to be somewhat stuffy, but the exact opposite is true. Emily Post was a lighthearted optimist and believed proper etiquette was a means for everyone to enjoy life to the fullest. She said, "Manner is personality—the outward manifestation of one's innate character and attitude toward life." Extending a thank-you is certainly one of the many ways to positively manifest yourself. This is a small sample of the thank-you letters that appear in chapter twenty-seven of *Etiquette,* entitled "Notes and Shorter Letters."

Letters of Thanks for Wedding Presents
Very Intimate

Dear Aunt Kate,

Really you are too generous—it is outrageous of you—but, of course, it is the most beautiful bracelet! And I am so excited over it, I hardly know what I am doing. You are too good to me and you spoil me, but I do love you, and it, and thank you with all my heart.

Mary.

Intimate

Dear Mrs. Neighbor,

The tea cloth is perfectly exquisite! I have never seen such beautiful work. I appreciate your lovely gift more than I can tell you, both for its own sake and for your kindness in making it for me. Don't forget, you are coming in on Tuesday afternoon to see the presents.

Lovingly, Mary.

For a Present Sent After the Wedding

Dear Mrs. Chatterton:

The mirror you sent us is going over our drawing-room mantel just as soon as we can hang it up! It is exactly what we most needed and we both thank you ever so much. Please come in soon to see how becoming it will be to the room.

Yours affectionately, Mary Smith Smartlington.

Thanks for Christmas or Other Presents

Dear Lucy:

I really think it was adorable of you to have a chair like yours made for me. It was worth adding a year to my age for such a nice birthday present. Jack says I am never going to have a chance to sit in it, however, if he gets there first, and even the children look at it with longing. At all events, I am perfectly enchanted with it, and thank you ever and ever so much.

Affectionately, Sally.

Dear Uncle Arthur:

I know I oughtn't to have opened it until Christmas, but I couldn't resist the look of the package, and then putting it on at once! So I am all dressed up in your beautiful chain. It is one of the loveliest things I have ever seen and I certainly am lucky to have it given to me! Thank you a thousand—and then more—times for it.

Rosalie.

The Bread and Butter Letter

When you have been staying over Sunday, or for longer, in someone's house, it is absolutely necessary that you write a letter of thanks to your hostess within a few days after the visit.

Examples

From a Young Woman to a Formal Hostess After a House Party

Dear Mrs. Norman:

I don't know when I ever had such a good time as I did at Broadlawns. Thank you a thousand times for asking me. As it happened, the first persons I saw on Monday at the Towns' dinner were Celia and Donald. We immediately had a threesome conversation on the wonderful time we all had over Sunday. Thanking you again for your kindness to me,

Very sincerely yours, *Grace Smalltalk.*

To a Formal Hostess After an Especially Amusing Week-End

Dear Mrs. Worldly:

Every moment at Great Estates was a perfect delight. I am afraid my work at the office this morning was down to zero in efficiency; so perhaps it is just as well, if I am to keep my job, that the average week-end in the country is different—very. Thank you all the same, for the wonderful time you gave us all, and believe me

Faithfully yours, *Frederick Bachelor.*

From a Man Who Has Been Ill and Convalescing at a Friend's House

Dear Martha:

I certainly hated taking that train this morning and realizing that the end had come to my peaceful days. You and John and the children, and your place, which is the essence of all that a "home" ought to be, have put me on my feet again. I thank you much—much more than I can say for the wonderful goodness of all of you.

Fred.

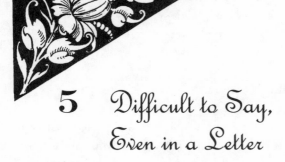

5 Difficult to Say, Even in a Letter

One of the hardest things in life is having words in your
heart that you can't utter.

—JAMES EARL JONES

Words are our allies and our enemies. Sometimes they show up on
call, just in time to make someone laugh or lend emotional aid when
it's needed. Other times they abandon us and we are left stuttering—
we can feel what we want to say but have no access to the means.

For the most part, the problem of coming up short is alleviated
when writing letters because you have ample time to think about what
you'd like to say. But there are certain circumstances when it's nearly
impossible to express genuine contrition or sorrow with mere words.
In these times, it's still important to take a deep breath and try. Unlike other letters that are difficult to write—such as breakup and
good-bye letters—because of how the reader will react, these letters
are a great challenge for the writer who may not even know where
to begin. In this case the writer needs to get over their insecurities for
the sake of the reader who wants—probably needs—words of comfort. In both apology and sympathy letters you have the daunting task
of looking for words that bandage a wound. You have a bit more control

over this when writing apology letters—since you were the one at fault; you are the one who can heal. With sympathy letters you do the best you can to let the other person know you're there.

APOLOGY LETTERS

Apologizing is a form of art. A masterpiece of an apology can completely alter the state of a relationship. The catch is you have to mean it. We've seen this scenario in sitcoms countless times: A man faces a woman and says, "I'm sorry." She asks, "For what?" He has no idea. Seriously, if you don't know why you're apologizing, then don't apologize. If you think you shouldn't have to apologize, again don't. Apologies only work if they're initiated with words and followed up by actions. Dishing out an empty apology just for the sake of pacifying the other person is only going to temporarily solve the problem. It'll be back. A genuine apology means you've decided what you did was wrong, you're willing to admit it, and also willing to work on it internally. If you apologize with words and not actions, then you will find yourself at square one again and again. Apologies, however, must begin with words—we can't skip straight to the actions. Whether spoken or written, we have to fully participate in the pride-swallowing ritual. Apologies on paper are straightforward and clear—they come close to being as perfect as possible.

I've written several apology letters, but it's a series of apologies I wrote after being fired for the first time in my life that stands out the most. I moved to New York City immediately after college in the summer of 2001 and was an intern at *O: The Oprah Magazine*. My interest at the time was fashion writing, so I worked in the fashion department. I learned quickly, there were not many writing opportunities for interns but lots of calling in and returning clothes for photo shoots. It was fun regardless, as I spent my days amidst designer dresses, sophisticated jewelry, and expensive shoes. Duties changed all the time and I was never sure what to expect. Toward the end of August, the fashion department was preparing for the forthcoming fashion week and I was assigned the task of making sure all the editors in my department were invited to the fashion shows. Here's how this works: Magazines have to call or fax design houses to let them know they're interested in seeing the collections. I was given a schedule of every runway show for that season. I knew the whens and wheres of Calvin Klein, Donna Karan, and Betsey Johnson, to name a few. This was by far my favorite assignment—I was a kid in a couture candy store. The market editor—a stylish, frank woman who I guessed to be in her late twenties—was the one person I hadn't worked with yet and she was directing me. She gave me the master list and highlighted every show I was to request tickets for. As I typed up the request letters on her behalf and faxed them out, I started to wonder about the shows that weren't highlighted—who gets to go to those? My curiosity and/or excitement must have been plain on my face as another editor passing by the fax machine asked me what I was doing. I told her and confessed that this list was one of the coolest things I had ever seen. After we spoke for a while, I snuck in my question about the shows that didn't make the cut. She gave me the greatest answer: "You could probably request tickets for yourself for some of those." I was hoping she'd say that! It had certainly crossed my mind, but that was the green light I was looking for.

When I went back to my desk to type up a fresh batch of letters, I wrote a few for myself. I explained that the market editor wouldn't be able to attend this season and she was sending me in her place. I am, by the way, laughing at myself right now. Really, what the hell was I thinking? I know what I was thinking: I had seen one too many movies about having to be sneaky and clever if you were ever going to leave the mailroom. Once I finished faxing, I was sent out to fetch bras and pantyhose for a photo shoot the next day. As soon as I got back, I walked into the market editor's office to give her a progress report and she cut me off immediately with "We have to talk about this." She was holding one of the notes I had written and forgot to fetch from the printer. Needless to say, she was not amused. She didn't yell, but still effectively drilled home that this was incredibly inappropriate and an embarrassment to both her and the magazine. Still blinded by my naïveté, I was surprisingly comfortable defending myself. I told her about the other editor with whom I had spoken at the fax machine. She told me it didn't matter, as that editor was not my superior. I explained that this was merely an attempt to learn about all aspects of the fashion industry. She told me had I been patient enough she would have taken me to a show. That comment frustrated me because I knew she didn't even know my name. We were both pretty determined—she to fire me and me to stand up for myself. When she finally asserted that this would be my last day, my attempt to swallow my tears was futile. If leaving the office in a mess of tears isn't humiliating enough, then not being able to hold back on the subway will humble anyone. As soon as I got home I called the assistant fashion editor who had hired me and who I worked with most often. She, of course, had heard the story by then, and I apologized frantically between deep breaths. She was sweet to say that she accepted my apology and was glad to have met me. That call was supposed to make me feel much better than it did. I had to do more. I sat down and typed eight individual, formal apology letters to the eight people I worked with: the creative director, market editor, beauty editor, assistant beauty editor, assistant fashion editor, assistant managing editor, accessories assistant, and my fellow intern. I dropped the letters off at the office the next day and walked away mourning my career in publishing, which was clearly a lost cause. The letters, to me, were the only way to salvage some shred of dignity. Admittedly, I can be very melodramatic.

My career picked back up the next day. I received a phone call from the editor who had encouraged me at the fax machine. She told me she was very sorry for the way things had turned out and she had a friend who hired interns at *Harper's Bazaar*. I started at *Bazaar* a week later and never ventured past calling in and returning clothes for photo shoots. A few weeks later I ran into the woman who fired me. I half froze when I saw her and didn't know whether to stand or run. She smiled at me and said, "Hi, Samara." If nothing else, I had accomplished one thing: she knew my name. Here are two of the eight letters I wrote. The first, is to the woman who hired me and the second to the woman who fired me.

The Apology Letters

AUGUST 29, 2001

Dear C——,

It is incredibly embarrassing for me to have to write this, but I know it is necessary. I am so sorry that I allowed my eagerness to cloud my judgment, and I cannot apologize enough for any disgrace I brought to *The Oprah Magazine*. I honestly did not realize the severity of the situation.

Above all else, I am so sorry to disappoint you. You have been so kind to me, and I was anticipating our continued work together. You told me yours was a thankless job, and somehow you muster up the energy to thank me and everyone else at the end of the day. I admire that, and I believe you'll infect this industry with courtesy someday. I promise in the future I will try and curtail my ambitions and wait for opportunities to present themselves to me. Thank you for all your advice, and, again, I am so sorry.

Best of luck, Samara

AUGUST 29, 2001

Dear P——,

I am truly embarrassed by my recent actions, and I regret placing you in such an awkward position. This is not an attempt to regain my status as an intern, but an offering of my sincere apologies. I am sorry for betraying the trust that was instilled in me and for any disgrace I brought to *The Oprah Magazine*. My actions were motivated by serious impatience, and I regret not being able to set that vice aside in order to make a better decision. I ask that you please try to understand that this was a mistake on my behalf and not something that was done with malicious intent. I am grateful for the time I did spend at *The Oprah Magazine*, and I assure you that I have and will continue to put a great deal of thought into my wrong-doing.

On a more personal note, I am so sorry for ruining the chance to get to know you and to work alongside you. Best of luck in the future.

Sincere regards, *Samara*

Be Specific

You need to know what you're apologizing for and explain how that came to be. Was it a misunderstanding? A bad day's frustration aimed in the wrong direction? Or were you just being a jerk?

> *How to Start*   First, swallow your pride. Then get right to it. However you plan to say it, "I'm sorry/I apologize/I'm completely worthless," it should go right up front and come no later than the second sentence. There's no need to beat around the bush, the sooner they know you're apologizing the better: "My behavior during the rehearsal dinner was completely unacceptable. First, let me apologize and then please let me explain." You could also open with a confession as to how you're feeling: "I am truly embarrassed by my recent actions," (as I did) or something like "I am humiliated by my impromptu drunken display at your birthday party."

> *From Here on Out*   Coming clean about what you did is important as is explaining what you're going to do to avoid the problem in the future. Sometimes it's a simple matter of figuring out how to avoid a misunderstanding: "Next time I'll listen

to your side of the story before I assume you went behind my back." If the problem runs deeper than a misunderstanding, a forward moving plan is certainly necessary: "My jealousy has gotten in our way many times before and now I'm willing to do something about it, as you've never given me any reason not to trust you."

Above all   What you should apologize for more than the action is the negative emotions the action resulted in: "I'm sorry we fought at the party, but more than that I'm sorry I embarrassed you." Or "It's not the lies I want to take back as much as the pain I caused you." "I know how stressed you've been recently and the last thing you needed was for me to add to it." If you're not necessarily sorry for what you did, but are very sorry for the way it affected the other person, then that's still an important part of an apology: "I'm sorry you thought my comment was out of line, and am so sorry it hurt your feelings. That certainly was not my intention."

Signing Off

It can be difficult to find a fitting ending for apology letters. Sometimes just signing your name is most appropriate, but if you'd like to give it a shot:

- *Apologies, apologies,*   A friend of mine ended an apology e-mail this way when she didn't answer an important question I had asked quickly enough.
- *With sincerity and chagrin,*   I once ended an apology like this and was fully forgiven.
- *Sincerely sorry,*   I find "sincerely" by itself to be trite and over-used, but when paired with sorry or "with sincerity," as above, it regains its meaning.

Grammar

I'll tell you something. The old-school computer I wrote these Oprah letters on did not have spell-check, and me without spell-check is embarasing. In my attempt to retrieve the letters for this book I e-mailed them to a new computer. As I opened the document I watched in horror as countless red lines came up. Five years later and this situation still makes me close my eyes and shake my head. I corrected my spelling here—I'm sorry. I had to! I'm sure they got a kick out of it: "Well, it's a good thing we got rid of her. She can't even spell!" If you're writing a professional apology, do as I say and not as I did and try to make them grammatically sound. As usual, personal letters can be a bit more lax.

How to Send

It doesn't matter. Get the message there as soon as possible.

If You Receive an Apology Letter

Try not to fight it too hard. If it moves you, then let it. If your acceptance of the apology is contingent on certain conditions, then put those out there and see if you can compromise. The ball is in your court now—just bear in mind that it will be your turn to apologize for something someday.

How to Apologize to a Girl for Getting Her Name Wrong in an Apology Letter

It's difficult to go untouched when faced with an apology letter. Even if you're content being angry, the effort on someone else's part is usually enough to snap you out of it. The apology letter below is one of the nicest I've ever received—written by a man I went out with once and didn't hear from again. It arrived in my e-mail account roughly two months after the fact. It's the type of apology most girls dream of, except for one miniscule problem: My name is wrong.

From: WhatWasHerNameAgain?@emailprovider.com
To: Samara@emailprovider.com
09/26/05 10:34 PM

Samantha—

I imagine I'm about the last person you're expecting to hear from. I definitely did quite a disappearing act. I'm writing to say I'm sorry. I didn't act the way I expected of myself, and it was very unfair to you. It was no reflection of you—I had a very tough summer, and I was in pretty bad shape. Not an excuse, by any measure, but at least an explanation. So for what it's worth, it was completely and utterly me. I think very highly of you, which is why I thought you deserved this email. I hope you're doing well.

I wasn't sure what to deal with first—the name thing or the apology thing. The name thing actually didn't bother me as much as I imagine it would bother most. People screw my name up all the time. It's Sa-MA-ra by the way—rhymes with Sahara. If that doesn't help try saying "The Good Samaritan" without "the good" and the "tan." Plus, the words after the name were pretty close to perfect. I've been blown off by plenty of men, not many of them attempt to apologize. I considered silently accepting the apology and not involving myself again, however, pointing out his mistake was irresistible.

From: Samara@emailprovider.com
To: WhatWasHerNameAgain?@emailprovider.com
09/27/05 4:07 PM

Actually, James Wolcott is the very last person I expected to hear from today, (I keep hoping he'll ask me to take over his column) but you come in a close second. Naturally, I would have liked for things to have worked out differently, but it is what it is. I hope things level out for you. Samara (not Samantha ☺)

From: WhatWasHerNameAgain?@emailprovider.com
To: Samara@emailprovider.com
09/27/05 9:31 PM

Oh dear god. Today-conscious-me wants to beat the CRAP out of yesterday-delirious-tired-coming-home-from-work-me. Now that I've officially humiliated myself, I have to leave New York. Great, I really like it here. I hear Uzbekistan is nice this time of year. (Two crazy things: 1) That wasn't a joke—I actually have heard that Uzbekistan is nice this time of year. 2) My friend went out with this Uzbek girl for a little while. Sort of a mix between Russian and Asian. Completely unintelligible accent, and yet he smiled and nodded constantly. Go figure.)

So, I will do ANYTHING to erase the mark from my already marred record. I can drop off an envelope of cash in your mailbox, but as I'm relatively poor—is there anything else I can do to redeem myself?

Can you keep a secret? I love this response—a clever blend of contrition and nervous humor. Admittedly, I'm a sucker. I fell right back in. Then a few days later I jumped right back out as I realized the word ANYTHING was pretty limited. I wanted him to call me and he was content disregarding that and making plans over e-mail, so our near reunion ended with the good-bye letter on page 32. I assure you, the fare-thee-well message had nothing to do with the comedy of error in my name—that continues to make me laugh. The apology letter itself still stands as one of my (and Samantha's) favorites.

How to Apologize for Missing a Lunch Date

I include this because I got such a kick out of it. My friend Mickey missed a lunch date we had planned—the hour came and went and I didn't hear from him. He's a very considerate person and promotes the standards of old-school etiquette—always walking closer to the street and standing up every time a woman gets up from the table. So when I didn't hear from him, I knew it was more likely that he'd been abducted than he was standing me up. Late that afternoon he called to apologize and I could hear how exhausted he was; he explained that work had gotten out of control. I told him it was no problem and we could reschedule. A few minutes later, he e-mailed me a formal, Emily Post–caliber apology:

From: Mickey@emailprovider.com
To: Samara@emailprovider.com
07/21/06 4:16 PM
Dear Samara,
I apologize for missing our get-together this afternoon. I haven't even had time to sip a glass of water. Hope to be back from Chicago Wednesday and will call then, Providence willing. A dinner treat is on me after you show me your offices when we next meet. Again, I'm sorry for today. Do have a fun cocktail hour and a lovely weekend.

Mickey

Never Too Late

There is no expiration date on apologies. They can be accepted days, weeks, months, and even years after the fact. Sometimes it takes that long for the offender to realize the severity of what they've done. I've been both the giver and receiver of apologies years later and they are extraordinary. I've tried to get myself in the habit of forgiving people whether they ask or not. If I don't, then I'm letting them weigh me down, and I can't have that. Perhaps the person whose forgiveness you'd like feels the same way or maybe they're on the brink of forgiving and all they need is for you to ask.

One of the Internet's greater amenities is it's made it remarkably easy for us to find each other. Don't be quick to assume that the other person has forgotten about the incident or that the belated confession would do no good. Chances are, if it still occurs to you, it still occurs to them. Joey, the boy you stood up in seventh grade because he wasn't popular enough, has most likely gotten over it, but the unsolicited apology could still brighten his day. Obviously not all cases are this light, but usually the harder the apology the greater the healing—for both people. The worst-case scenario: They don't forgive you. That's not ideal, but it's okay—take great comfort in the fact that you've forgiven yourself.

How to Apologize to Your Husband for Being Short with Him as the Housework Continues to Mount

BY KATHERINE MANSFIELD (1888-1923)

Kathleen Mansfield Beauchamp was born in Wellington, New Zealand. She was educated at Queen's College in London and went on to become a renowned short-story writer. She toyed with a number of pen names and eventually settled on Katherine Mansfield. Always looking for trouble in younger days, she had a number of love affairs and abruptly married a teacher named G. C. Bowden at the age of twenty-one, then left him the same evening. In autumn of 1911, she met the man she'd be with the rest of her life—critic John Middleton Murry. He was the editor of a magazine called *Rhythm* and fell in love with her short story "The Woman at the Store," which he published, before he fell in love with the woman herself.

Although they wanted to be, they weren't technically married because Bowden (husband for a day) didn't grant Katherine a divorce until 1918. The two had lived together for little more than a year when this letter was written, and it seems that was the time when the romance was dying down and the routine setting in. They were going through what most couples go through: Katherine is frustrated with the housework and frustrated with Jack for expecting her to do it—then she apologizes for being so easily frustrated. Katherine died at the age of thirty-five of tuberculosis, and Jack went on to publish a volume of their letters. Jack's nickname for her was Tig. He explained: "The name Tig by which she signed, and by which I called her, grew out of a joint signature which we used for some articles on the theater in 'Rhythm'. We signed them, 'The Two Tigers.'"

MAY/JUNE *1913* (UNCERTAIN OF THE DATE)
'THE GABLES,' CHOLESBURY

Am I such a tyrant—Jack dear—or do you say it mainly to tease me? I suppose Im a bad manager & the house seems to take up so much time if it isn't looked after with some sort of method. I mean . . . when I have to clean up twice over or wash up extra unnecessary things I get frightfully impatient and want to be working. So often, this week, Ive heard you and Gordon talking while I washed dishes. Well, someone's got to wash dishes & get food. Otherwise—"there's nothing in the house but eggs to eat." Yes, I hate hate HATE doing these things that you just accept as all men accept of their women. I can only play the servant with very bad grace indeed. Its all very well for females who have nothing else to do . . . & then you say I am a tyrant & wonder because I get tried at night! The trouble with women like me is—they can't keep their nerves out of the job at hand—& Monday after you and Gordon & Lesley have gone I walk about with a mind full of ghosts of saucepans & primus stoveses & "will there be enough to go round" . . . & you calling (whatever I'm doing Tig—isn't there going to be tea. Its five o'clock.) As though I were a dilatory housemaid! I loathe myself, today. I detest this woman who "superintends" you and rushes about, slamming doors & slopping water—all untidy with her blouse out & her nails grimed. I am disgusted & repelled by the creature who shouts at you, "you might at least empty the pail & wash out the tea leaves!" Yes, no wonder you 'come over silent'.

Oh, Jack, I wish a miracle would happen—that you would take me in your arms & kiss my hands & my face & every bit of me & say "its alright—you darling thing, I quite understand." All the fault of money, I suppose. But I love you & feel humiliated & proud at the same time. That you dont see—that you dont understand and yet love me puzzles me————

Will you meet me on Wednesday evening at the Café Royale at about 10.30. If you can't be there let me know by Wednesday morning . . . Ill come back and sleep at '57' if I may even though I don't live there. Jack—Jack—Jack

Your wife Tig

SYMPATHY LETTERS

Undoubtedly the most difficult situations in which you're called to offer comfort are those surrounding death. At first, there always seems to be no words. I've found though that once the initial shock and sadness pass, a plethora of memories breaks through and that's where you can get your words from—from the person who has gone.

My story of a sympathy letter comes from a death I still don't understand. It was one of my very good friends from high school, Megan. She and I got to know each other while doing stage crew for *The King and I* our freshman year and were inseparable until we were seniors. We weren't that great at keeping in touch when we went to college, but when we managed to meet up over breaks it was always wonderful, as if no time had gone by. I heard about her through the grapevine too—I knew when she got her MA and when she got married. She's one who always makes me happy when I think about her.

Megan died unexpectedly at the age of twenty-five. I found out through e-mail. There's something about e-mail that's still not real to me. Sometimes when I make plans over e-mail, I'm not always sure the other person will show up. So my first reaction was not to believe it, but then I thought who would pass along such horrible information if it wasn't true? My mother called later that day to tell me it *was* true. There's something about my mother's voice that's very real, and I lost it. I cried until I couldn't see straight, as if I had just seen Megan yesterday. When my tears simmered to sniffles, I went home and pulled out pictures of Megan and with those spread out around me I wrote to her mother. I sent the pictures and the letter overnight. Days later as I walked through the receiving line, I saw my letter posted between all the pictures.

The Sympathy Letter

May 2005

Ms. Lemke,

I am shocked and devastated at the sudden loss of your beautiful daughter and my once very good friend Megan. I am praying for you in this time of trial and am certain that you will derive strength from the same place that Megan always did: from God himself.

Although Megan and I have lost touch over the years, her memory is strong with me. I remember well the endless laughter that she would implement with quirky inside jokes. I remember wishing I had her sense for fashion and jewelry. I remember late nights up at camp and the two of us sharing our sixteenth birthday together. She and I were two very tall girls who always felt a little awkward about it and always managed to convince each other that we were still okay because of it. I was so proud of her as she plowed through school, so she could meet her end goal of helping less fortunate people.

You raised your daughter to be strong, kind, and above all faithful. We may never know why God decided to take her from us at such a young age, but we should trust he has a reason and he'll let us in on it someday. Ms. Lemke, you're in my thoughts and prayers and please let me know if you need anything at all.

In deepest sorrow, Samara

Be Specific

In the name of timeless advice, I leave you, again, in the hands of Emily Post: "Intimate letters of condolence are like love letters, in that they are too sacred to follow a set form. One rule, and one only, should guide you in writing such letters. Say what you truly feel. Say that and nothing else. Sit down at your desk, let your thoughts dwell on the person you are writing to."

How to Start It's difficult to say exactly how to begin a sympathy letter. It depends so much on the situation and if it was sad yet expected or absolutely tragic. It really is about saying what you feel. If you're indescribably sorry, say that. If you can't find the words, you can say that too. In her book *Dear Pussycat: Mash Notes and Missives from the Desk of Cosmopolitan's Legendary Editor* (St. Martin's, 2004), Helen Gurley Brown starts off two sympathy letters in very different and equally moving ways. The first was written to a woman who's husband died after a prolonged illness: "I can't believe Steve isn't with us—he was one of the most dynamic forces God—or whoever creates things—ever put on earth—wasn't his life astonishing? The life force inside your husband was like none

I've ever seen in any other person and it touched us all again and again." The other was written to a couple whose son was murdered: "I usually can write letters—it's what I *do*—but I was so horrified by what happened to Jonathan I just couldn't think of anything adequate to say. I still can't, although I know you must be grieving deeply and inconsolably."

🖋 **If You Knew The Person** Let your letter be a celebration of them and what they brought to your life. If you haven't seen them in years, then old memories work just as well. Perhaps if it was a friend's mother: "My memories of your mother will always be as warm and wonderful as the treats she made for us."

🖋 **If You Didn't Know the Person** Let your letter be centered on the person who is grieving and their relationship with the deceased: "Although I never met Karl, I always got a kick out of your stories about him and his hunting trips. I could see how happy he made you, and I am so very sorry for your loss."

🖋 **Beaming with Pride** If you've been privy to privileged pride once admitted by the deceased, now is a good time to come clean about it: "I know we've only met a few times, but I feel as if I've known you for years as your father was always bragging about you."

Signing Off

✉ **My condolences, In sympathy, In deepest sorrow,** Traditional closings for condolence letters.

✉ **With love and prayers, Blessings, May God be with you,** If you take a religious approach.

✉ **All my love, Your friend, Lots of love,** You can certainly break with tradition and end the letter giving a simple token of your own personal affection.

Grammar
Write what you feel, and however it comes out is fine.

How to Send
Please avoid e-mail at all costs here, unless it's really the only way you can get the message to them. If ever there was a time to splurge on FedEx and UPS to make sure your note arrives tomorrow morning, this is it.

Religious Context

In the face of death, it's hard to know what is and isn't appropriate as far as belief systems go. Megan and I were part of the same youth group and I knew her mother was very active in her church, which is why I was comfortable being so forthright with spiritual assertions. If you don't know where the person in mourning stands on the religious plane, it's still usually fine to tell them they're in your thoughts and prayers, as most people don't take offense but appreciate the sentiment. If you know the person to be an adamant atheist, then perhaps it's not a good idea to mention prayer as it might upset them more. If you yourself have no religious affiliations then it's fine to tell someone they're in your thoughts, let there be no pressure to mention prayer. Following the death of my mother's sister, a friend of hers at work said, "I know someone who can contact her for you." My mother, the last person to believe in communicating with the dead, simply said, "Thank you, but that's okay."

How to Express Genuine Regrets to a Woman who Lost Five Sons During the Civil War

BY ABRAHAM LINCOLN (1809–1865)

Portrait of President Lincoln first published in 1861

Often grouped together with his other exceptional writings, such as the Gettysburg Address and the Second Inaugural Address, is Abraham Lincoln's sympathy letter to Mrs. Lydia Bixby—a widow living in Boston said to have had five sons die on the battlefield during the Civil War. There is great debate concerning this letter, as it was later found that Mrs. Bixby only lost two sons to the war while one received an honorable discharge and the other two may have been deserters. It has also been called into question as to whether Lincoln himself wrote this letter—some speculation suggests it was written by John Hay, private secretary to the president. Regardless of the controversy, whoever wrote the letter, wrote it under the assumption that these five brothers died fighting for their country and the letter itself lives on—an extraordinary set of words written around an especially tragic situation.

NOV. 21, 1864

EXECUTIVE MANSION, WASHINGTON

Dear Madam,

I have been shown in the files of the War Department a statement of the Adjutant General of Massachusetts that you are the mother of five sons who have died gloriously on the field of battle. I feel how weak and fruitless must be any word of mine which should attempt to beguile you from the grief of a loss so overwhelming. But I cannot refrain from tendering you the consolation that may be found in the thanks of the Republic they died to save. I pray that our Heavenly Father may assuage the anguish of your bereavement, and leave you only the cherished memory of the loved and lost, and the solemn pride that must be yours to have laid so costly a sacrifice upon the altar of freedom.

Yours, very sincerely and respectfully, A. Lincoln

6   Letters of Change

If not us, then who? If not now, then when?
—JOHN LEWIS (SAID DURING THE CIVIL RIGHTS MOVEMENT)

Human beings are as predictable now as they've always been. The constant craving for money and power has never really been satisfied but are continually sought after. The futile hunt for these two things accompanied by an intrinsic fear of change, repeatedly leads to corruption and the denial of even the most basic rights to countless people. In many devastating cases, people are not even entitled to their own opinion.

The seemingly flawless tactic that imperialists have always implemented is to ensure that the masses, or sometimes a select group of citizens within the masses, remain uneducated. Ignorance equals compliance. The one factor that is almost always left out is the human spirit. The only desire that rivals the desire to dominate is the deep-seated desire for justice. As history has shown us time and again, when small voices dare to shout, things start to change.

LETTERS REQUESTING ACTS OF AMNESTY

If you're like me, charity work is something you really want to do—someday. Someday when you're older and not working so hard, when you have more time and money to spare. You'd really like to help make a difference for someone somewhere, but now is the time to look out for you. Then it changes to the time you have to look out for your spouse, then eventually your children. Soon you come to realize that day is not coming. No one is handing you a time ticket saying, "Okay you're free for a while, go off and save the world." As John Lennon once sang, "Life is what happens while you're busy making other plans." If philanthropic work is something you (by you, I mean me) really want to do, then the time has to be consciously set aside. Fortunately, there is an effective, altruistic act that doesn't require much time or money. It requires good intentions, which I believe most of us already have.

Here's what you do: Pick a cause, any cause, and find (by find, I mean Google) the letter-writing campaign attached to it—the odds of there being one are very good. The research is done for you. All you have to do is read, agree, and send a letter. Many campaigns have an e-mail option, although most emphasize that print letters are still more effective. It takes two extra seconds to cut and paste the letter, print, and mail. I've tried to get myself into the habit of sending both ways. Use the form letters at first, and when you become more familiar with the cause then feel free to articulate your opinion with your own words—always respectfully. Make sure when you send a form letter that you read and agree fully with everything that's written. Send one a month, one a week, one a day if you're up for it. It's inexpensive, and again, effective.

The Nobel peace–prize-winning organization that has launched an exuberant number of full force letter-writing campaigns is Amnesty International (AI). AI was founded in 1961 by a British lawyer named

Peter Benenson. He was reading the paper one day and was disturbed to discover that two Portuguese students had been imprisoned for a term of seven years because they had raised their glasses in a toast to freedom. Benenson wrote to the editor of *The Observer* requesting readers write letters on their behalf. The response was tremendous and soon letter-writing groups were formed in more than a dozen countries. AI is still standing strong as one of the most revered human rights organizations in the world with its main goals to free prisoners of conscience—anyone imprisoned because of their race, religion, color, language, sexual orientation, or belief, so long as they have not used or advocated violence—and to raise awareness about human rights abuses.

I first encountered AI when I was in college and campus ministry had agreed to work on a few campaigns. I remember thinking writing letters was way too easy to have any substantial effect. I thought of AI again when I added a links page to my Web site—if letter writing could make the world a better place, then I should be promoting those types of letters too, yes? This thought was followed by the two-seconds-too-late-you-flake revelation that if writing letters could make the world a better place I should be *writing* those types of letters. AI has several campaigns to choose from, including controlling arms and denouncing the torture of prisoners. One prominent campaign that I gravitated toward immediately was Stop Violence Against Women. The description reads: "Currently, Amnesty International is involved in an international campaign to stop violence against women. Every day, women and girls around the world are threatened, beaten, raped, mutilated, and killed with impunity."

It's easy for us to take our rights for granted. Of course we should enjoy and be grateful for them, but we need to remind ourselves that most of the women in the world have no such rights and that American women certainly did not always have them. The following is the first letter I wrote for this campaign. For the most part I stayed with the provided form letter but added a few thoughts of my own (in italics). AI is still working to see this bill pass.

The Letter Requesting an Act of Amnesty

Dear Governor,

I welcome the current discussion of a "Domestic Violence and Other Related Matters Bill," by the Lagos House of Assembly. In Nigeria, women suffer from violence in the family: they get 'punished' for supposed transgression, beaten, raped, or murdered. *Home is where one finds refuge and strength; it should not be a place where women suffer and fear to go.* The Bill, if passed, will help to protect women who face violence in the family.

The government of Lagos State, along with the federal government of Nigeria, have obligations under international human rights law to prevent violence against women and to assist women in escaping violence. Perpetrators must be prosecuted, and victims of violence given full support. As the Governor of Lagos State, you have the power to make a difference for these women. *Women are the world's most undervalued resource and once given the opportunity to reach their full potential, they will prove their worth ten times over.*

I urgently ask you to voice your support for the "Domestic Violence and Other Related Matters Bill" and undertake a thorough public education campaign on this issue. I urge you to publicly condemn violence against women: say it is never normal, legal, or acceptable and that it is a human right abuse. Thank you for your attention to this important matter.

Yours sincerely, Samara O'Shea
New York, NY, USA

Letter-Writing Guide for Amnesty International USA and the Urgent Action Network:

I will stray from my usual format here and leave you in the hands of the experts. AI carefully researches each of their campaigns and brings otherwise unknown injustices into the spotlight. You are in the safe hands of accomplished peacemakers when you choose to write on behalf of any of their causes.

Why write letters? It's simple. It works.
Letters can . . .
Free a Prisoner of Conscience (POC): "I am writing to inform you that after 6 years, 4 months, 17 days in prison, I am now free. I walked out of the prison gate . . . with my shoulders unbent, with my head unbowed. I feel great to be free again, to walk, once again, in the sunshine of freedom." —university lecturer in history and former POC, Maina Wa Kinyatti, Kenya

Strengthen an individual: ". . . Messages of solidarity that have been sent to me from many parts of the world, reach my cell. It feels like every time a letter of solidarity arrives, the rose in my cell blossoms. This is a very warm feeling." —POC, Dita Sari, Indonesia

Stop torture: "You are not dead, because too many people are concerned about you." —a security agent to a political prisoner, Argentina

Improve prison conditions: "We could always tell when international protests were taking place . . . the food rations increased and the beatings were fewer. Letters from abroad were translated and passed around from cell to cell . . ." —A released POC, Vietnam

Tips for Effective Letter Writing
Use Shortcuts

Do whatever is necessary to make your letter writing as quick and easy as possible. This way, letters will not be put off and they can be sent out sooner. Start by making a generic file for each type of concern; paragraphs on torture, the death penalty, disappearances, denial of medical care and so on, can be copied into your working file and edited as needed. You may find it useful to refer to the sample passages on [page 122] to get your letter started and shake "writer's block."

Salutations

There is no international standard for addressing authorities. These formalities vary according to different governmental structures in each country. Urgent Actions and other AI appeals will usually give you a suggested form of salutation for each official. In general, you may safely use:

- *Your Majesty* to kings, queens, and other monarchs.

- *Your Excellency* to all heads of state, cabinet-level ministers, prime ministers, ambassadors, and governors.

- *Your Honor* for judges and procurators.

- *Dear Sir/Madam* for local authorities, prison commanders, police chiefs.

- *Dear Admiral, General, Captain, etc.* for military officials.

Closings

Close your letter in a formal style by using:

- Respectfully, or Yours respectfully,

- Sincerely, or Yours sincerely,

- Yours truly,

If You Have Writer's Block . . .

Writer's block happens to the best of us. Keeping a file of your messages can help give you a jumping-off place to start a new letter, by providing inspiration. Below are some phrases and sentences that may also help get you writing again when your mind draws a blank, but remember to use them only as suggestions—it is always better to use your own heartfelt language.

Starting

- "I wish to appeal to you on behalf of _____, who is the subject of my deepest concern . . .

- My family and I are worried about _____, who is reportedly detained unjustly in your country . . .

- I am dismayed to hear that _____ has received several death threats recently.

- I would like to take the opportunity to call your attention to the case of _____ . . .

- We are calling on you to ensure the fair treatment of _____ . . .

Ending

- . . . I hope to hear from you in the very near future.

- . . . I, and all here who share my concern, would appreciate a reply from you as soon as possible. Our concern for the basic rights of individuals in your country is not of a political nature, it is simply a concern for the dignity and well being of all humans.

- . . . Thank you in advance for your time on this urgent matter.

- . . . Finally, in view of the above information, we urge you to act quickly to remedy this situation and ask that you inform us of the outcome of your investigation.

DEATH THREATS TO A UNION LEADER

I was concerned to learn of recent death threats made against _____, a member of the United Confederation of Workers in Colombia on August 4. She was told that she would be killed for her trade union activity. I urge you to ensure that a full and impartial investigation is made into the threats, that the results are made public, and that those responsible are brought to justice.

TORTURE OF STUDENT LEADERS

I was gravely concerned by reports of the arrests of a number of student leaders at the University of _____ in October. I was particularly concerned that some of the detainees, who are being held at the _____ Detention Center, are reported to have been tortured and I seek your assurances that these students and other detainees held at _____ will be treated humanely.

DEATH IN DETENTION AND "DISAPPEARANCE"

I am writing to express my concern over the reports of the death in custody of _____, following his arrest in Baku on January 19. I urge an immediate investigation be conducted into the circumstances of his death and that results be made public. At the same time, I write to ask you for information on _____'s whereabouts, who was also arrested on January 19, and I seek assurances that her physical safety be guaranteed while in detention.

How to Send Your Appeals

E-MAIL

It is extremely easy to send your appeals via e-mail and costs you nothing but time and care. A problem with e-mail, however, is that many government officials either do not have e-mail addresses or do not make their e-mail addresses known to the public. Thus, Amnesty actions will not always list e-mail addresses for all government officials. If you receive your Urgent Actions via e-mail, you might find it useful to cut and paste brief portions of the action into your own message. *However, please do not send or forward the original Urgent Action directly to the official.* A message composed by you that reflects your concern written in your own words will be the most effective. Carefully consider how you compose the subject line of your e-mail: it should encourage the official to open your e-mail, so be polite and thoughtful when choosing your words. For example: "Asking for Your Help to Find Roberto Daman Lopez." If you want to forward the Urgent Action itself to a friend, colleague, or fellow Amnesty International activist, please send the complete text of the Urgent Action as it was sent to you without editing its content.

FAX

Most actions will include the fax numbers of one or more government officials. This is an immediate, fairly inexpensive way to communicate your concerns to governments. Because your faxed message is received as it appears, you can send petitions with signatures. You can use a letterhead that will help to individualize your appeal and make it more effective. The cost of sending a fax is the cost of a short international phone call. A fax message can be a full-length letter since it is so inexpensive to send (in contrast to a telegram or cable). You should consider including your fax number in your message and request a faxed reply from the official. If you do not have a fax machine at your home or office, many local print shops will allow you to use theirs for a fee. A variety of Web-based companies will send your e-mailed appeal as an international fax. One such service provider is Faxaway at http://www.faxaway.com (phone: 1-800-906-4329). You should check with your own Internet service provider for others.

TROUBLESHOOTING FOR E-MAILS AND FAX

Problems with fax numbers and e-mail addresses often exist. When a government official's fax or e-mail is listed on an Urgent Action that is distributed globally to activists in over 80 countries, you can imagine how many faxes and e-mails begin to come in to the official's office. This often results in the official's e-mail or fax being turned off for a period of time. Officials may even permanently discontinue service for that address or number. For faxes, another problem may arise when inadequate phone lines in the country of destination sometimes thwart international calls. A persistent busy signal or bounced e-mail message may mean that other activists are faxing or e-mailing in their appeals, which is a good thing! Have patience and keep trying. If you cannot get through on an e-mail address or fax line for a long period of time, please airmail your letter so that the official hears your concerns in a timely manner.

AIRMAIL

Sending an airmail letter to a government official is sometimes the most feasible way of communicating your concern about a victim of human rights abuse. When fax numbers and e-mail addresses do not work, or if you do not have access to a fax machine or the web, consider sending an airmail letter. Ideally, your letter should be one page and include your signature and return address so the official can respond to your concerns. Airmail postage rates often change. The current rate, as of July 2005, is eighty cents for one ounce (one page letter with envelope) to most countries; to Mexico and Canada: sixty cents. You can always check the international postage rate for specific countries and types of delivery at http://ircalc.usps.gov/. Postcards are also highly effective. Postcards cost seventy cents to most countries, fifty cents to Mexico and Canada. You can buy pre-stamped postcards at the post office. If you buy them elsewhere, be careful about the image on the front of the card; do not choose anything which might be deemed disrespectful or inappropriate to postal workers, government officials, or anyone else in the country where you are sending it.

TELEGRAM/CABLE

A telegram is an expensive way to send your appeal, however, it can offer an effective method of getting the attention of an official. In terms of cost, telegrams and cables should be thought of as a last resort, utilized because of the extreme nature of the case. We suggest that you send your appeal as a telegram only at times when the situation is particularly urgent and as your group's or your own budget allows. Telegram cost is calculated per word. Since abbreviations and punctuation such as commas and periods count as words, omit them and all unnecessary words and articles whenever possible. The text of the telegram should be short and to the point. The signature should include your name and mail or e-mail address so that the official can respond to your appeal. Here is an example of the truncated language used in telegrams (also called cables).

EXTREMELY CONCERNED ABOUT NEWS REPORTS HERE THAT _____ HAS BEEN PLACED IN ISOLATION AND DENIED FAMILY AND LAWYER VISITS. PLEASE ALLOW MORE HUMANE TREATMENT OR UNCONDITIONALLY RELEASE HER NOW

(Approximate cost of this telegram sent to Cuba: $85.00.)

There are several companies that can send a telegram for you. You may find a listing of them in the "Telegraph Services" section of your local Yellow Pages directory.

Beyond Letters
VARIATIONS ON AN URGENT ACTION APPEAL
Once you have the basics down for writing an effective letter, the possibilities are endless. Letter writing can and should be creative and fun.

While the largest portion of AIUSA's Urgent Action Network is made up of individual letter writers, all Amnesty International community groups and student chapters receive monthly Urgent Actions. Urgent Action appeals can be sent as:

- Postcards to officials

- Letters to the editor in your local paper

- Telegrams/Faxes

- E-mails

- Petitions

- Prewritten letters to circulate at a local farmer's market, town festivals, faith group meetings, retirement homes, coffee shops, and brew pubs

- Local radio station broadcasts

Note: This guide has been printed only in part. For the complete letter-writing guide and a current human rights case to write a letter on, contact:

Urgent Action Network
Amnesty International USA
600 Pennsylvania Ave. SE, 5th Fl.
Washington, DC 20003
Phone: (202) 544-0200
Fax: (202) 675-8566
Email: uan@aiusa.org
Web: http://www.amnestyusa.org/urgent/

To find out more information on AIUSA's volunteer opportunities or programs, visit www.amnestyusa.org or call the AIUSA Regional Office nearest you at 1-866-A REGION.

How to Write the Women's Right's Revolution

BY ELIZABETH CADY STANTON (1815-1902) AND

SUSAN B. ANTHONY (1820-1906)

Elizabeth Cady Stanton with her daughter Harriot in 1856

Daguerreotype of 28-year-old Susan B. Anthony

One might think that by the early twentieth century, it'd be a given that women would get the right to vote—the "it's about time" attitude should have kicked in. Not so. Suffragists and anti-suffragists both fought tooth and nail until the very end, as they had for seventy-two years.

The first women's rights convention was held in Seneca Falls, New York, in 1848. A thirty-two-year-old woman named Elizabeth Cady Stanton stood up and made the outlandish suggestion that women should be given the right to vote. The room of 300 women and forty men erupted into shock and disagreement. I say it here and it sounds sarcastic, but it was that extreme. Women in 1848 had no rights. They had no rights to their property, to their earnings, or to their children. There was no legal recourse for a woman who had been the victim of domestic abuse. With no rights in the home, to suggest that women enter the political arena was especially radical. The crowd disagreed vehemently on suffrage until abolitionist Frederick Douglass (1818–1895) came to Stanton's aide by standing and agreeing with her. Then it began.

Two years later, Stanton met a Quaker woman named Susan Brownell Anthony, and the two formed a fast friendship that lasted the rest of their lives. The forward thinkers fought fervently to convince both men and women that women had the intellectual capacity to handle voting. Disappointingly, much of the opposition came from anti-suffragist groups organized by women, to whom Stanton said, "It is too bad that these women are begging to be left in their chains."

Anthony remained unmarried and campaigned across the country for suffrage and was in constant correspondence with Stanton, a mother of seven, who cheered her on and helped her write speeches from home. In 1872, Anthony voted illegally in the presidential election. She was arrested and tried. Because she was a woman she was not allowed to testify on her own behalf. The judge did not allow the all-male jury to convene—he ordered them to proclaim the defendant guilty. She was told she had to pay the 100-dollar fine plus the court fees. Her response to this was: "May it please your honor that I shall never pay a dollar of your unjust penalty. Resistance to tyranny is obedience to God." Tragically, neither of the women lived to see the suffrage movement succeed. They did, however, lay a rock-solid foundation without which women gaining the vote in 1920 would not have been possible.

I'm sure you've gathered by now that I like to read old letters, but it's rare that I read letters more than 100 years old that affect my life directly. These do. They affect every single one of my rights, not the least of which is my right to write this book. In these exchanges, their exhaustion is evident and giving up is a constant temptation. Thank God, they didn't! Ladies, thank you for your shoulders. We're still standing on them.

APRIL 2, 1852
SENECA FALLS, NY

My dear friend (Susan B. Anthony),

I think you are doing up the temperance business just right. But do not let the conservative element control. For instance, you must take Mrs. Bloomer's suggestions with great caution, for she has not the spirit of the true reformer. At the first woman's rights convention, but four years ago, she stood aloof and laughed at us. It was only with great effort and patience that she has been brought up to her present position. In her paper, she will not speak against the fugitive slave law, nor in her work to put down intemperance will she criticize the equivocal position of the Church. . . .

I will gladly do all in my power to help you. Come and stay with me and I will write the best lecture I can for you. I have no doubt a little practice will make you an admirable speaker. Dress loosely, take a great deal of exercise, be particular about your diet and sleep enough. The body has a great influence upon the mind. In your meetings, if attacked, be cool and good natured, for if you are simple and truth-loving, no sophistry can confound you. As for my own address, if I am to be president it ought perhaps to be sent out with the stamp of the convention, but anything from my pen is necessarily radical no one may wish to share with me the odium of what I may choose to say. If so, I am ready to stand alone. I never write to please anyone. If I do please I am happy, but to proclaim my highest convictions of truth is always my sole object. . . .

I have been re-reading the report of the London convention of 1840. How thoroughly humiliating it was to us! . . . . Men and angels give me patience! I am at the boiling point! If I do not find some day the use of my tongue on this question, I shall die of an intellectual repression, a woman's rights convulsion! Oh, Susan! Susan! Susan! You must manage to spend a week with me before the Rochester convention, for I am afraid that I cannot attend it; I have so much with all these boys on my hands. But I will write a letter. How much I do long to be free from housekeeping and children, so as to have some time to read, and think, and write. But it may be well for me to understand all the trials of a woman's lot, that I may more eloquently proclaim them with the time comes. Good night.

*Dear Mrs. Stanton,

How do I long to be with you this very minute, to have one look into your very soul, and one sound of your soul stirring voice—

How are you, and how comes on the letter for the National [Women's Right's] Convention? It seems impossible to array our forces for effective action this Autumn. I, therefore, a few days since, wrote Lucy Stone, begging her to Postpone the Convention into May next. . . . That Convention has been a heavy burden from me, the last two months. Nothing looked promising. Nobody seemed to feel any personal responsibility and [I], alone, feeling utterly incompetent to go forward, unless sure of the reliable and effective speakers to sustain the Con., could but grope in the dark. But I now hope Lucy will say amen to any proposition. . . . I can't Remember whether I have answered your last letter or not. Be that as it may, I will remember how good a word it brought to me, and how it cheered me onward. Mrs. Stanton, I have very weak moments, and long to lay my weary head somewhere and nestle my full soul close to that of another in full sympathy. I sometimes fear that I too shall faint by the wayside, and drop out of the faithful few.

There is so much, mid all that is so hopeful, to discourage and dishearten, and I feel alone. Still I know I am not alone, but that all the true and the good souls, both in and out of the body, keep me company, and the Good Father more than all is ever a host in every good effort. But you will see that this is one of my tired moments, so no more, but to the Cause thereof.

I left home the [?th] of Sept., and commenced Anti-Slavery work at Binghamton. Had three weeks of cold hard labor among people not initiated into the first principles of true freedom. I returned home the 19th Sept. found company there, and company came and came . . . For a week I was in such a home whirl. On Friday the 25th I left for Collins Progressive Friends Meeting . . .

---

*Portions of this letter have been left out. The remaining words have not been altered.

Mrs. D. from the Committee read a paper on Women's Rights going back to Women's position in marriage as the starting point. Mr. *Davis spoke first. He set forth his idea of the nature of the sexes and their relation to each [other]. Spoke truthfully and nobly of re-production, of the* abuses *of marriage etc, etc. But to his idea of the sexes, he said women's inherent nature* is Love *and* Man's Wisdom. *The Love reaches out to Wisdom, Man, and Wisdom reaches out to Love, Women, and the two meet and make a beautiful blending of the two principles. . . .*

My soul was on fire. This is but a revamp *of the world's idea from the beginning, the very same doctrine that consigned woman from the beginning to the sphere of the affections, the subjugated her to man's wisdom. . . . The question was* called *for. I* must out, *and said Mr. President, I must say a word, and I did say a word. I said* Women. *If you accept the theory given you by Davis, you may give up all talk of a change for women: she is now where God and nature intended she should be. If it be a fact that the principle of Wisdom is indigenous in Man, and Love an exotic, then must wisdom* prevail, *and so with women, must* Love *prevail.*

Therefore women must look to man *for* Wisdom, *must ever feel it impossible for her to attain Wisdom equal to him. Such a doctrine makes my heart* sink *within me, said I. And did I accept it, I would return to my Father's house, and never again raise my voice for woman's right to the control of her own person, the ownership of her own earnings, the guardianship of her own children. For if this be true, she ought not to possess those rights. She ought to make her final appeal to the wisdom of her husband, father and brother. My word stirred the waters, and brought Davis to his feet again, but he failed to extricate himself from the conclusions to which his premises philosophically lead. Well Sunday, there were more than* a thousand *people congregated, hundreds more* out *than in doors. . . .*

All day yesterday, the likeness and the unlikeness of the sexes has been the topic of discussion . . . The discussion has been loud and long, and how I wished you *could be here. I tell you Mrs. Stanton, after all, it is very precious to the soul of man, that he shall* reign supreme in intellect, *and it will take Centuries if not ages to dispossess him of the fancy that he was born to do so . . .*

I must add that many women came to me and thanked me for the word I uttered in opposition to Davis. Said they, had you not spoken we should have gone home burdened in soul.

Oh Mrs. Stanton how my soul longs to see you in the great Battle field. When will the time come? You say in two or three years. God and Angels keep you safe from all hindrances and keep you from all mountain barriers. If you come not to the rescue, who shall. . . . ?

Don't fail to write me. It always does me so much good to get a letter from you. A kiss for Maggie and Hattie and Sadie and a kindly word for the boys. . . .

The Letter That Changed It All

On January 10, 1918, the Susan B. Anthony (nineteenth) amendment had finally made it to the House of Representatives. It was short, but it was thirty-nine words that would change everything: "The right of citizens of the United States to vote shall not be denied or abridged by the United States or by any State on account of sex. Congress shall have power to enforce this article by appropriate legislation." It passed by a 304 to 90 vote in the house and went on to win a 56 to 25 vote in the senate. To become law it would have to be ratified by thirty-six states.

The cause was one state away from victory when the devastating news came that Delaware had defeated the amendment. The next state in line was Tennessee—suffragists feared a southern state would never rule in their favor. In the summer of 1920, both sides of the movement descended on the unsuspecting city of Nashville. It appeared as though suffrage would lose by one vote.

One of the votes that was a guaranteed nay was that of republican Harry Burn. At twenty-four years old he was the youngest member of the Tennessee legislature and a known anti-suffragist. Days before the decision was to be made, he received a letter from his mother saying that if it came down to him, he should help put the "rat" in ratification.

On August 18, 1920, Harry Burn, wearing a red rose (the sign of anti-suffrage), astonished the press and the peanut gallery and voted that women should vote. And so we do.

LETTERS TO THE EDITOR

In the fall of 2005 I attended the Pennsylvania Governor's Conference for Women (pagovernorsconferenceforwomen.org) in Philadelphia. It was an extraordinary daylong event with more than 4,000 women in attendance to discuss current issues. The keynote speaker roster was remarkable—Governor Ed Rendell had invited Madeline Albright, Sandra Day O'Connor, and Lisa Ling to impart their wisdom and experience to a keen crowd. At the end of the day a questionnaire was passed out to find out what we thought of the event and to assess how politically active we are. One of the questions denoting our political participation was "Have you written a letter to the editor recently?" I perked up proudly and checked yes, as I had learned the week before that a letter I wrote to *Vogue* would run in the November issue. I'm sure *Vogue* was not the publication they had in mind and my letter did not illustrate an opinion they cared about one way or the other, but I appreciated that they cited writing letters to magazine and newspaper editors as an important device in staying publicly active. Letters to the editor are the quintessential forum for readers to connect with the publication as well as with the public. They exemplify the crux of democracy—being allowed to have an opinion and express it without fear. Magazines and newspapers show their true colors on the letters page—a publication that runs letters both in and out of its favor is one that truly values reader's opinions.

The letter I wrote to *Vogue* was on the out-of-its-favor side—it was slightly out of the magazine's favor but more so out of Madonna's favor. Before I continue, I must come clean about what a ridiculously dedicated

Madonna fan I am. It all started when I was allowed to stay up and watch the 1989 MTV music awards. She opened the show and my infatuation began. I know adolescent celebrity crazes are supposed to die down with time, but mine never did. My fixation has always frustrated my mother—Madonna's most vocal critic—who asked me tersely one day, "What is it exactly that you like about her anyway?" I didn't hesitate to answer, "Her ambition." I'd backed my mother into a parental control corner, "Oh, well that's okay," she said.

Like all relationships, however, even the celebrity/fan relationship has its problems. I was reading the August 2005 *Vogue* and Madge was the cover story. Somewhere in the middle of the story she was quoted: "I don't read newspapers. We don't read magazines. No television. At the end of they day they're all noise." I've heard Madonna say repeatedly that she does not watch TV, but this was the first time I saw it extended to newspapers and magazines. *Is she making fun of me?* I thought. *Am I not holding a magazine? Is she not on the cover?* I was talking to a friend about it later who said she thought the same thing. It was her opinion that inspired me to write the letter, wondering if we weren't the only two people who thought that. I e-mailed it a few days later and in the next two weeks *Vogue* wrote back to say they would print it. My letter certainly wasn't going to move any mountains, but it made me feel better and I was pleased that they valued my viewpoint.

As the publication date grew closer, I developed a ridiculous fear that I would offend my idol. I knew she wouldn't read it (after all, she doesn't read magazines) but perhaps her publicist would. It was unlikely but not impossible. I eventually put this out of my mind and accepted all I was doing was using the media to express my opinion. I'd like to think Madonna, of all people, might appreciate that.

The Letter to the Editor

NOVEMBER 2005

I am a loyal Madonna fan and an avid VOGUE reader. I was, however, frustrated with both as I read the August issue. In it,

Mrs. Ritchie proudly boasts that she doesn't bother with newspapers, television, or magazines, because "at the end of the day they're all noise." I'm curious as to whether or not she includes her own music videos, live performances, album reviews, and sitcom appearances in this arbitrary "noise" category.

Madonna's career would not exist without these media. I agree at times they can be trashy. But they can also be informative and insightful. How else did she plan to get the word out about Kabbalah? Her hypocrisy is off-putting and I wish VOGUE had called her on it.

Samara O'Shea
New York, NY

Be Specific

I got a little cocky with my beginner's luck, as this was the first letter to the editor I had ever written. I enjoyed seeing my name in a magazine that I couldn't yet write for otherwise and thought, seeking the same thrill, I'd try to write to other trendy magazines. This was futile, and none of those letters were ever published. It didn't take long for me to decide it's ridiculous to write without purpose. Respond to the articles and issues that move you—those pieces you can't stop thinking about because of the way they're written or what is said. It doesn't have to be earth-shattering; it could be a recipe you enjoyed or a project you tried. As long as your motivation is genuine, being specific is easy.

How to Start When you find yourself moved, the hardest thing to do is condense your thoughts, but your letter stands a much better chance of being published if it gets right to the point. Editors have the rest of the publication to edit so a reader letter that arrives in concise, quality form is welcome with open eyes.

Do Them a Small Favor In the name of making it easier on the editors, include the name and date of the article you're referring to in parentheses ("Along These Lines," July

2006). It's a small task but it keeps them from having to do it and is undoubtedly appreciated.

🖎 ***Know the Publication*** Some publications, especially newspapers, allow for longer letters. Note the format on the letters to the editor page of which you are writing, and if they're willing to print slightly longer letters, then give it a go. Try not to go too far over the word count of the longest letter they've run. If you find your letter becoming extremely lengthy, it might be a contender for a newspaper's op/ed page instead.

🖎 ***DON'T SHOUT*** If something angered or upset you, don't write in all capital letters. Also, don't rant and rave needlessly. State your frustration in a matter-of-fact and respectful way. Publications are usually willing to admit they have run something wrong, but they don't respond well, understandably, to aimless tirades.

Signing Off
Most publications do not print any sign off, they just publish your name, city, and state. If you choose to sign, you can use any standard professional closing such as:

✉ ***Sincerely, Warm regards, Yours truly,*** but know it will most likely be cut. Only if you're writing to Dear Abby do you have to come up with some clever emotional declaration such as, "Thoroughly Confused in Massachusetts."

✉ ***Respectfully,*** A good way to end a strongly worded letter. It let's them know you're frustrated/offended/etc. but you appreciate that they're taking the time to consider your insights.

Grammar
If it's going to print, most publications will correct your grammar for you, but not always. Some publications, usually facetious men's maga-

zines, reserve the right to ridicule their readers all in good fun. Again, know the publication you're writing to and take note of how they respond to reader inquiries. To be on the safe side, keep your grammar as clean as possible. Remember, once you send the letter it belongs to the publication and they can do with it what they will.

In the early days of my career, I worked as an editorial assistant at a magazine and was in charge of compiling the reader mail and choosing the letters that would be published. With that in mind, if your grammar is plain embarrassing and your argument falls short of making any sense, it will be passed around the editorial office and made fun of. Just so you know.

How to Send
E-mail or fax. Unless it's going to a magazine with a small circulation, print letters are likely to get lost in the mix. You can usually find out the circulation on the publication's Web site under "media kit." If the publication does not have a Web site, it has a small circulation. Be sure to read the e-mail requirements carefully, as many magazines request you include a daytime phone number for fact-checking purposes and will quickly dismiss your letter if they see you didn't include one.

Missing the Mark

Don't take it personally if your letter doesn't make it to print. The odds that it won't are good, as there are thousands, sometimes millions of readers out there and one tiny letters page. I've written two (genuinely motivated) letters that I was sure would run and didn't. The first came a few weeks after the Madonna letter. I walked to the newsstand and Paris Hilton was there to greet me, as she usually is, except this time she was greeting me topless and from the cover of *Vanity Fair*—the only magazine I subscribe to. *Not you guys too?!* I wrote my strongly worded letter the next day and sent it off. They were kind enough to get back to me not to tell me my letter was running but rather to assure me that they had received a multitude of similar letters. That warmed my heart, and it was a testament to the fact that just because a letter doesn't get printed doesn't mean it goes unheard. I didn't make it onto the letters page but I did make it into the *Vanity Fair* mailbag—a summation section of all the letters they don't have room to print usually found at the end of the all the letters. I think I made it in there as I started my letter with "Et tu *Vanity Fair?*" and that question was listed in the mailbag regarding Miss Hilton. If it came from another reader, I'm with you, man.

The second letter I was sure would run was to *The New Yorker.* Now I'm not one who walks around thinking I have any valuable insights to lend that establishment of a publication, but in early June 2006 they did a story on my good friend Stephen Joyce (adversary of erotic letters) and it seemed too good to be true as I had received a letter from him about a month prior. I was looking forward to joining the community of writers whose projects had been thwarted in whole or in part by Stephen "James" Joyce (as he prefers to be called). I wrote to thank them for their article, told of my experience, and pointed out that time is ultimately on our side as Joyce's work gets closer to being in the public domain every day. The letter didn't run. *Oh come on!* I thought. *How many of your readers actually have a letter from the bitter grandson?* When the response issue did run, all three of the letters to the editor were in reaction to that piece (*The Injustice Collector,* June 19, 2006) and were decidedly more scholarly than what I had written.

How to Tell Americans What It's Like to Live in the Middle of World War II

BY THE EDITORS OF FRENCH AND BRITISH *VOGUE*

The last place one might think to look for a war update would be the pages of a fashion magazine, but these letters, printed in the July 15, 1940, issue of American *Vogue,* offer a candid look no visiting reporter could ever capture—as they are written by the people who were experiencing the war firsthand. Although the United States had not yet entered World War II when these letters ran, Americans were still sympathetic to the suffering that was taking place in Europe. Mailed from the frequent Nazi bomb targets of Paris and London, here are the testimonies of the editors and contributors of French and British *Vogue* written as they lived amidst terror and tragedy. These letters, sent to Edna Woolman Chase—American *Vogue*'s editor in chief from 1914 to 1951— serve to show that war makes exceptions for no one regardless of class and status.

Letters from France and England

Vogue's friends write us or telephone us every day to say—"What about French *Vogue*—what about British *Vogue*?" To those who are interested or fearful about the well-being of our staffs across the sea—to all interested in the welfare of anyone across the sea—these letters have a special interest.

JUNE 5, 1940 LETTER FROM JOHN MCMULLIN, AT HOTEL DU PALAIS, BIARRITZ

Mr. McMullin used to write, "As Seen by Him," a column in Vogue *on the activities of the international set. Since the war began, this set has given time, money, and work to France until ordered to evacuate Paris.*

Dear Edna: Biarritz at this moment is a strange site . . . so many Rolls Royces, maids, valets, and dogs gathered together under so few roofs. This hotel has a list of people that reads like the "Grand Semaine" at Deauville in the old days.

Meanwhile Paris is being bombed. We know no details but are waiting to hear how close to our villa the bombs fell. My chauffeur-valet leaves in a few days to serve his country. He is the young man who drove you to the Abbey for the Coronation.

We Americans over here, who have belonged to the so-called international set, now seem to be of a completely old-fashioned era. That stuff is so outdated.

Here at the Biarritz, people seem to be strangely quiet at the moment. But one may be sure they won't always be so. And then what is going to happen? Certainly, these rich fashionables will never live like that again. John

JUNE 5, 1940 LETTER FROM LADY STANLEY, OF ALDERLEY, ON *VOGUE*'S LONDON STAFF

Dear Mrs. Chase: As you can imagine, it is hard to write at all these days. I have just walked back from Whitehall through St. James's Park—a mass of purple iris and all the railing taken away for scrap-iron so that it looks like a private garden. I walked a little way with a Colonel who has just flown over from Le Bourget and describing the bombing of Paris. Apparently, it was horribly accurate.

The anxiety among my friends during the last few days has been dreadful— wondering if their husbands were saved or not. But everyone is calm and uncomplaining. A tremendous fighting spirit has been awakened. If parachute men flap down from the air, I am sure the women in the country will turn into Scarlett O'Haras.

My little house is crammed with people; soldiers turn up unexpectedly from Dunkirk and need places to rest for a few days. All they want to do is sleep, they are so dead tired. The ordeals some of them went through were dreadful, but they seem full of fun and jokes and want to fight again at the earliest opportunity.

Only the big new placards are in print now, and they just say LATEST WAR NEWS. The news bits are marked in chalk on slates or written in blue pencil on paper—because the news changes so quickly.

Only the weather cheers us—Yours very sincerely, Audrey Stanley

JUNE 7, 1940 LETTER FROM DUCHESSE D'AYEN, FASHION EDITOR OF FRENCH *VOGUE*

Dearest Edna: Thank you, thank you with all my soul and heart, you and all the dear friends of Vogue. *Owing to your immediate and generous relief check, we shall relieve so many pathetic people. It breaks your heart to see them; old peasants, old women, children, leading their great Percheron horses, trudging away from their homes as in Biblical times, without shedding a tear. The whole scene is so cruel, so deeply tragic.*

More than ever, American help means everything to us and American generosity is absolutely wonderful. Every moment of sympathy and belief in the

cause for which we are fighting; every gesture, every dollar, every cent, is helpful. To us, on borders of the Seine, and not so far from the battle, loves, lives, and belongings have lost every kind of value. There is only one aim——succeed.

The great fight we are watching is much more than a war. Listening to the statements of warriors coming back from the North, one gets the whole picture. Men on a beach facing death on one side and the wide ocean on the other——the limit of the world.

Of course, we suffer and we shall suffer more——the price matters no more. Thank you for all . . . Solange d'Ayen

JUNE 11, 1940 LETTER FROM AUDREY WITHERS, MANAGING EDITOR OF LONDON *VOGUE*

Dear Mrs. Chase: It is so difficult to edit here these days. We try to look at each sentence sideways and imagine how it will read in the face of all the disasters that may happen before it sees the light of day. The situation changes with terrific speed.

We are trying to think how we shall operate if we must move to Richmond. The stumbling block may be distribution——the general opinion seems to be that the first effect of prolonged air raids would be to disorganize transport.

We are working on the Wool Expert supplement. And do try to do what you can to help stimulate the importation of British Wools into America——it will help vastly.

Everyone in the office is marvelously calm. Our art editor had to give up his house at two days' notice——that whole area has been commandeered for troops. But we are all well. Love, Audrey Withers

7   If We Must, We Must

No editor can ever afford the rejection of a good thing,
and no author the publication of a bad one.
—THOMAS HIGGINSON (EDITOR OF *THE ATLANTIC MONTHLY*
IN "LETTER TO A YOUNG CONTRIBUTOR" IN APRIL 1862)

The epigraphs that have started each chapter thus far have been self-explanatory, but for this one I'll clarify. I'm willing to bet editors—working in magazines, books, film, television, etc.—reject good ideas on a regular basis because they're presented poorly. It's easy to cast something aside when, at first glance, the margins are off, the punctuation bad, and one word, let alone several, is spelled incorrectly. The good idea is masked behind its messy appearance and unfortunately, lost for good. This is true, not just of editors, but anyone in a hiring position—they overlook stellar candidates all the time because the presentation is bad. If you are said stellar candidate or are writing a recommendation for that person and know that you (or they) could excel at a particular job, then it's important to know your weaknesses when it comes to written forms of communication and go out of your way to overcome them. Have your friend the English teacher read all of your letters and your brother-in-law the graphic designer format your résumé. Make sure you are as good on paper as you are in person.

BUSINESS LETTERS

Since they are an infinite number of reasons for writing a business letter, I'm going to include the most common—cover letters, resignation letters, and professional thank-you notes. We'll deal with cover letters first since they are the most widely used form of professional correspondence and still written formally, whereas most other business transactions take place informally over e-mail nowadays.

Cover letters are the first impression. Even if you have access to the CEO through a good friend, it's still important to demonstrate your organizational and communicative skills in your cover letter. It's true that some employers prefer what the résumé says to what the cover letter says, but since you never know if this is true, it's best to make them both outstanding. The cover letter below was my standard cover letter a few years ago. It didn't get me the job at *Lifetime* magazine I was applying for, but it did eventually get me a few job offers and some freelance work. On a side note, *Lifetime* magazine folded after a year. I'm an advocate of the cliché that everything happens for a reason, especially when it comes to job hunting. Every job I have *really* wanted that didn't work out has been better for me in the long run. So don't be too disappointed if you don't get your dream job—you will, and the job you didn't get probably wasn't right for you anyway. Another opportunity will come along.

The Cover Letter

SEPTEMBER 29, 2003

Dear Ms. Buchan,

I am writing to you with great interest in the assistant editor position at *Lifetime* magazine. Due to downsizing I have recently left Hearst magazines as an assistant to the lifestyle editor at *Country Living Gardener*. The magazine's intimate setting and small staff allowed me to participate in a variety of tasks—making me a skilled and versatile candidate.

My background includes writing and editing feature stories, producing decorating stories, assisting with product photo shoots, updating Web copy, and an array of related responsibilities. I am acquainted with myriad computer programs and research tools. I have included my résumé along with writing samples and would be happy to provide references upon request. Thank you for your time and I look forward to arranging an interview.

Cordially, *Samara O'Shea*

Be Specific

But don't be too specific. During my internship at *Harper's Bazaar*, I came across a cover letter that one of the other interns had saved to the desktop of our common computer. It was all about her dreams. I can't quote it verbatim, but the first paragraph detailed how she had hoped, prayed, and wished upon every single star that she would someday come to New York and work for a magazine. She let the recipient know that, if they hired her, they'd be fulfilling all of her childhood aspirations. Yeah, employers don't usually care about your dreams. They're interested in your skills and how you acquired them. In a similar, more recent situation, a friend of a friend asked me to read her cover letter—she was applying to *Good Housekeeping*. She let the managing editor know that she had fond memories of her mother's copies of *GH* sitting on the coffee table. Again, that's nice but obvious and not necessary. Also, both of these letters were full pages single-spaced—entry-level candidates have no business writing cover letters that long. A one-page letter, double-spaced will suffice. If it falls shorter than a full page, which it should, that doesn't mean you have less to offer, it means you know how to get to the point.

> *How to Start* Begin by stating your purpose: "I am writing in regards to the manager position posted on Monsterjobs.com." "I am writing to you with great interest in the marketing coordinator position."

📎 **Name Dropping**   If you have a name to drop, now is a good time. "I heard of this opportunity through David Stroup. He and I were in the same fraternity at Penn State."

📎 **Where You Are Coming From**   "I am a recent graduate of New York University." "I've just returned from a year abroad." "I am currently working at Worthington Inc."

📎 **What You Can Do for Them**   Next, tell them how the place you're coming from has equipped you for the next challenge (i.e. the job you're applying for): "As an associate at Worthington I've been able to master codes, databases, and programming." This may be a paragraph or more depending on your experience.

📎 **Offer Your References and Suggest a Follow-up**   Most people say their references are available upon request, but it's not unheard of to enclose or attach a letter of reference or two. Then end on an optimistic note indicating contact in the near future. "I'll call you within the next few days." "I look forward to arranging an interview." "I'd like to elaborate on my qualifications in person, and hope to schedule a time we can meet."

Signing Off

✉ **At your command,**   Christopher Columbus (1451–1506) signed a letter this way as he was reporting his discoveries in the Caribbean back to the monarchs and other officials—Columbus thought he was writing from India.

More modern closings include:

✉ **Cordially,**   My favorite.
✉ **Sincere regards, Best regards, All the best, Yours truly,**   Take your pick.

✉ **_Many thanks_,**   Another favorite.
✉ **_Sincerely,_**   Overdone, but reliable.

Grammar

Flawless. Yes, flawless. Never send these without having at least one, preferably two, people (who know something about grammar!) look it over. Grammar is language that not all of us speak and even if you do speak it, there will come a point when you've read your letter so many times that your eyes glide right over the mistakes. Even if you're in a hurry to send it, have someone else look it over.

The frustrating thing is the management person you send this to probably won't give it a good read—they'll skim it. But God forbid they catch their eye on the word you spelled wrong or the comma you forgot, because that will make the rest of the letter obsolete.

How to Send

If you're sending a cover letter then it's best to e-mail or fax. However, if you e-mail, write a quick introductory sentence and then attach your cover letter and your résumé. It's best not to cut and paste your letter and résumé because the format can get screwed up from one computer to the next. Also, opening an e-mail and seeing an in-depth cover letter might be irritating to the recipient, whereas if it's attached they can read or print it on their own time. An introductory e-mail can read: "Dear Mr. Holz, It was a pleasure meeting you Monday night at ESPN Zone. Thank you for sharing your valuable insights on working for IBM and the Dallas Cowboys. I have attached my cover letter and résumé for your consideration." If you have a name to drop, you can do it here rather than in your cover letter. If you haven't met the person and have no name to give, then this sentence can simply state the facts. For example, "Dear Mrs. Briney, Attached pleased find my cover letter and résumé regarding the public relations associate position with the San Diego Chamber Orchestra."

The Resignation Letter

Resignation letters are the last word. It's always best to leave a job on the up and up. Even if you've been fired, it can benefit you to write and apologize that things turned out the way they did but you were grateful for the time you did spend there. If you're giving your resignation, you should tell them in person and hand over the typed letter for the company's records. If you know your company is very formal and expects the letter first, then your decision is made. I wrote this for one of my customers (names have been changed).

JANUARY 2006

Dear Francine,

I am writing to you to offer my official resignation from Mullins effective Friday, January 27, 2006. I have enjoyed my work experience immensely, but as my family continues to grow I've decided it's best for me to be a full-time parent. I cannot say enough wonderful things about Mullins, about all the people I've worked with, and especially about you. Your leadership skills are exceptional and you have taken our department to a higher level. I have also appreciated both the personal and professional advice you have kindly given me. It's my hope that we will stay in touch as I begin this new chapter in my life. I have given a little more than two weeks notice and hope this time is sufficient. Thank you again for everything.

Warm regards, *Sally Henries*

Professional Thank-you Notes

Although professional thank-you missives have fallen to the wayside, never underestimate their power. They can be the catalyst for creating stronger business binds and can certainly make you stand out. The only time I think professional thank-you notes are absolutely necessary is following a job interview. However, they are certainly welcome at other times—thank you for the bonus, thank you for the extra vacation days, thank you for the promotion. As far as saying thank you, I still say a handwritten note trumps all others. However, I know many people who've sent an e-mail thank-you following a job interview and it was well received. When thanking someone after a job interview try to add one anecdote that steps aside from business and gives a little insight into your personality. Don't go overboard with this, one will do. The first example below is a thank-you following a job interview (for myself), and the second is thanks for another great year (for a customer):

APRIL 2004

Dear Ms. McGee,
Thank you for taking the time to meet with me and go over the details of the assistant home editor position. It sounds like an exciting challenge, especially working on the home almanac pages. This opportunity comes at a perfect time for me, and I am pleased to be considered. Thank you again for your time and for letting me see the Ansel Adams prints in your office—an impressive collection! I hope to be in touch soon.

Warm regards, Samara O'Shea

DECEMBER 2005

Don,
I hope you and your family have had a good year and that you're excited for the upcoming one. My year was exceptional, thanks in large part, to my job, which continues to be a source of joy for me. I know I've mentioned this before, but I wanted to reiterate how I enjoy working for you. You never make me feel as though I work for you but rather with you and

I greatly appreciate it. I am flattered that you confide in me, and I'm eternally grateful to you for giving me stock in the company before we went public. As a result, my husband and I have been able to attain an unimagined level of financial standing. Thank you for sharing your talents with all of us! And, as always, thank you for the generous gift basket. Happy Holidays!

All the best, *Linda*

How to Approach a Problem in a Businesslike Manner

This was a fun assignment. One of my customers came to me and said her daughter had volunteered at the APT Masters Tennis Tournament in Cincinnati, hoping it would count toward her community volunteer hours. (The school requires each student to accumulate a certain number of hours.) She was very disappointed when her teacher told her this type of volunteering wasn't hands-on enough and wouldn't count. I was glad Mrs. Martin (as we'll call her) wanted to write a formal letter addressing the situation. The traditional approach—mom going to talk to the teacher—can oftentimes be disastrous. Mom, of course, thinks her child deserves the world and the teacher, naturally, has her own standards to uphold. So if Mom walks in after school one day asking (sometimes demanding) that her child be given credit, then the teacher's defenses automatically go up and the two adults can quickly become two children. I'm not saying this is how it would have gone, but it's possible. Many parents are smug in thinking they'll just talk to the teacher and everything will be fine. Instead, Mrs. Martin asked me to write a letter laying out all the reasons this situation served as a learning experience for her daughter.

A proper, professional approach to common situations can make them more agreeable to all parties. A friend of mine tells a great story about how her boyfriend wanted to go to a boarding high school and his parents said absolutely not. He did extensive research on the subject as well as the school he wanted to attend and presented it to his parents. Impressed by his maturity, they let him go. A written plan of action for many situations such as borrowing money from a friend or family member will most likely have a similar effect on the recipient. As for the community service hours, Mrs. Martin said they were gladly approved.

JANUARY 24, 2006

Dear Mrs. Lang,

I am writing on behalf of my daughter, Jessica Martin, with the hopes that you will consider her work as a ball girl at the ATP Masters Tournament in July and August 2005 to count toward her community volunteer hours.

I know events of this nature are not usually accepted, but I assure you Jessica worked very hard and learned a great deal. I believe there are two elements that constitute a truly advantageous volunteer experience. The first is self-discipline, which is a must for doing any work that you don't get paid for. The glamour of the tournament wore off quickly for Jessica and the long hours, extreme heat, and fatigue set in. She realized though that this was a commitment she had made and had to follow through with.

The second essential element comes with knowing that the work you are doing is for the benefit of a greater cause. In this case, there were two causes. The direct cause was the Cincinnati Children's Hospital—the tournament has raised money for the hospital for the past thirty years. The indirect cause was the city of Cincinnati itself. The tournament is an annual event that is counted on to bring in tourism and economic prosperity. In the grand scheme of things Jessica's contribution may have been small, but it was also necessary. The tournament cannot function properly without the help of those willing to volunteer. I ask you to recognize and give her credit for both her time and effort. Thank you for your consideration.

Cordially, *Anne Martin*

How to Secure a Business Deal that Will Educate the Masses

BY ANDREW CARNEGIE (1835-1919)

A portrait of the quintessential self-made man, photographed by Marceau, New York

This letter is neither a cover, resignation, nor professional thank-you. It is, however, one of the most remarkable business transactions to take place via letter and I had to include it. Andrew Carnegie, the son of a hand-loom weaver, was born in Dunfermline, Scotland. The family to moved to Allegheny, Pennsylvania (now part of Pittsburgh), as a result of the depression of 1848 in Britain. Young Andrew worked in a cotton factory for $1.20 a week. He later worked as a desk clerk and attended night school to study bookkeeping. In 1853 he was working as a telegraph operator when Thomas A. Scott moved to Pittsburgh as division superintendent of the Pennsylvania Railroad. Scott was so impressed with the 18-year-old, he hired him as his personal clerk. Six years later, Carnegie was division superintendent. In 1865, he turned his attention to the expanding iron industry and spent the next thirty-five years building Carnegie Steel into an abundant enterprise. In March 1901, he sold the company to J. P. Morgan, which on completion, provided him with $225 million in bonds. Not one to forget his modest beginnings, Carnegie focused on philanthropy the rest of his life. Days after the Morgan sale, he wrote the following letter to J. S. Billings—director of the New York Public Library—announcing a forthcoming, incredible donation. Carnegie went on to endow more than 2,800 libraries across the country.

NEW YORK 12TH MARCH 1901

Dr. J. S. Billings,

Director New York Public Library

Dear Mr. Billings,

Our conferences upon the needs of Greater New York for branch Libraries to reach the masses of the people in every district have convinced me of the wisdom of your plans.

Sixty-five branches strike one at first as a large order, but as other cities have found one necessary for every sixty or seventy thousand of population the number is not excessive.

You estimate the average cost of these libraries at, say, $80,000 each, being $5,200,000 for all. If New York will furnish sites for those Branches for the special benefit of the masses of the people, as it has done for the Central Library, and also agree in satisfactory form to provide for their maintenance as built, I should esteem it a rare privilege to be permitted to furnish the money as needed for the buildings, say $5,200,000.

Sixty-five libraries in one stroke probably breaks the record, but this is the day of big operations, and New York is soon to be the biggest of Cities.

Very Truly Yours,

Andrew Carnegie

RECOMMENDATION LETTERS

Being asked to write a recommendation letter is flattering. It means the person requesting the reference thinks highly of you and your accomplishments and they're hoping you can help them achieve their goals. Writing recommendation letters can be fun as you examine your working relationship with the petitioner and aide in helping them step up to the next level. Keep in mind that recommendations say as much, if not more, about you as they do about the person you're endorsing. If you make false claims and say they're organized when they're not or that they're punctual and they are far from it, then this reflects just as poorly on you. It's best to only write testimonials on behalf of those you think competent and capable. This is different from just liking someone. You can like someone very much but know that they don't have it in them to be a White House intern or to succeed in medical school. It's okay to be honest and up-front about this, as a misleading recommendation might hurt both of you in the long run. Luckily, this is usually not the case as most people have a good sense of their rapport with teachers, employers, clergy members, and anyone else they might think to ask for a reference.

I wrote the following recommendation letter for one of my customers who couldn't say enough nice things about the friend she was advocating. The friend was applying for a position as a federal judge and needed several letters of reference. In the end, she did not get the job, but I'm sure there were many factors, not this letter alone, that went into that decision. As usual, all the names have been changed.

The Recommendation Letter

NOVEMBER 22, 2005

To Whom It May Concern:

I would like to recommend Ingrid Crawford without reservation for the position of federal judge. I have known Mrs. Crawford for the past ten years, and she is an ambitious woman of the highest moral conviction and character.

I met Mrs. Crawford when she was the President of Junior League—I was instantly moved by her passion for volunteering and community. Subsequently, I was impressed by her leadership skills and effectiveness as a public speaker. I proudly watched as she excelled as an assistant prosecutor and served two terms as a judge on the common pleas court.

On a personal note, Mrs. Crawford has been a reliable friend as well as a visibly wonderful wife and mother. She has a sound Christian faith that inspires all of her decisions. Ingrid Crawford is sure to bring her spirited set of family values and commitment to any position that she holds. If you'd like to discuss her attributes further, please don't hesitate to contact me.

Cordially, *Carol Saville*

Be Specific

You can go a little overboard with the adulation, as it's not yourself you're selling here. Just make sure that every superfluous point leads back to something substantial. For example, "Since she was a child, Julia has talked about her dream to own a bookstore and I was amazed that she was savvy enough to pull it off in her early 20s. This is true of all of her undertakings—when she sets her mind on something, she always follows through."

How to Start   Start off with stating clearly what you're recommending the person for and then move right into how long you've known them and how you met them. If you haven't known them that long, you can use that to your advantage, "Zachary has worked for Cold Stone Creamery for a little more than five months now, and in that short time he has impressed me with his outstanding customer service skills and increasing sales numbers."

Mention One Flawless Flaw   Make the crux of the letter about the person's attributes and mention one flaw that's not really a flaw. I find "doesn't like to ask for help" is a good one. "Has been known to work too hard" or "is distracted by obtaining perfection" can also work.

✍ **On a Personal Note** Round off any recommendation letter with some comments on the person's character. In recommending them you're saying they're a hard worker and more than capable of the tasks at hand, but this extra piece attests to them being a pleasure to work with also. The phrase "on a personal note," is the written equivalent of stepping away from the podium and looking someone in the eye. You're pulling them aside to say, "No really, I like this guy a lot."

Signing Off

If you know the person to whom you're writing, then it can be an informal closing, otherwise end as you would end any other professional note with **sincerely, cordially, all the best, etc.**

- ✉ *I remain, sir, Your obedient servant,*
- ✉ *Your truly obliged,*
- ✉ *Yours most sincerely,*   All per *Collier's Cyclopedia,* 1892 (You'll read about in at the end of this section).
- ✉ *Cheers,*   A more casual closing. At first, it bugged me when non-British people would use Cheers, but I have since warmed up and find it endearing.

Grammar

This letter will be read more carefully than most formal letters. Remember, recommendation letters say as much about you as the do the person you're recommending, so you want them to be as clean as any professional letter you'd write on your own behalf.

How to Send

It depends on your relationship with the recipient. If you're an old friend or former colleague, then e-mail is perfectly acceptable. If you don't know the recipient, then it should be typed, printed, and formatted as any other professional letter.

If Someone Writes a Recommendation on Your Behalf

Write them a thank-you note—especially if you get the job or get into the school or are permitted to adopt a child, etc.

How to Politely Refuse to Write a Recommendation

Easy, no. Necessary, sometimes. It could be as simple as someone wanting a reference for an upcoming job and you've never actually worked with the person, or they're asking you to attest to their parenting skills as they seek to adopt and you've never seen them within fifty feet of a child. Naturally, this task can be more daunting when you have worked with someone and know him or her to be less than adequate. If you're a teacher and a lackluster student is asking for a recommendation, what you might do is tell them you have a personal policy of only writing two (or however many) references a year, to ensure that's there's appropriate enthusiasm in each letter. Here are some suggestions on how to word your refusal.

> "Although I've known you for years, we've never worked together and I can't give an accurate account of your work ethic. If you ever need a personal recommendation, I could go on and on about your many wonderful attributes."

> "Please accept my apology, but I don't feel comfortable confirming your capacity as parents as I've never seen you around children. I am certain that you are wonderful with them and will find someone who can go on about this better than I."

> "I've seen many improvements in your work this year, but I know that you are still far behind your potential. Once you reach the heights I know you can, I'll be the first to write about them for you."

◐ "Due to some of our professional disagreements earlier this year, I don't feel as though I'm the best person to recommend you for the management position. I apologize if you see this as unfair, but I think you'll benefit much more from someone else's testimony."

How to Write a Recommendation Letter for Your Offspring

A friend of mine was writing an article on how to get into college for a teen magazine. She interviewed several admissions counselors who provided helpful tips. One counselor told a horror story of a student who came equipped with twenty-two letters of recommendation, including one from her mother. This, of course, is ridiculous. Anyone would roll their eyes at a reference letter from a parent, unless the school requested one. I hadn't heard of this until one customer came to me and said the private high school her daughter was applying to wanted a parental letter of recommendation. That's a clever way to size up the personality of the parents, I thought. Kelley (as we'll call her) was accepted to the school. I'll tell you, as I told her mother, it's hard to write an exceptional letter without an exceptional candidate. This was easy to write:

DECEMBER 20, 2005

Dear Ms. Mason,
I am writing on behalf of my daughter, Kelley Davis, requesting that she be considered for acceptance to Jesuit High School. Understandably it's difficult for a mother to be objective about her daughter, but I'll do my best to paint an impartial picture.

Kelley is an intellectually and athletically ambitious young woman. She has been on the honor roll consistently throughout grammar school. She enjoys being a member of the student government as well as singing in the choir. She is an avid soccer and basketball player and looks forward to participating in both on her high school teams.

On the flip side, Kelley will put off schoolwork for the sake of a good book any day. It's difficult for me to discourage her from reading so much, but her schoolwork must come first. She also doesn't like to ask for help. She prefers to figure things out on her own, which hasn't been a huge problem so far but I'm afraid it will be as her studies become increasingly difficult.

My husband and I look forward to being full participants throughout Kelley's high school career. Whether this means helping with homework, attending every soccer and basketball game, or donating time and money to charity events we are happy and excited to oblige.

I believe an education founded on the principles of the Jesuit order will benefit Kelley immensely. She will leave Jesuit High equipped with the tools and moral convictions she needs to excel in college as well as the work force. She would certainly be a lively and gifted addition next fall, and I hope you'll consider admitting her. Thank you for your time.

Cordially, *Cindy Davis*

How to Write Recommendation Letters

ACCORDING TO *COLLIER'S CYCLOPEDIA OF COMMERCIAL AND SOCIAL INFORMATION* (1892)

Books on etiquette and the best ways to live your entire life were once a dime a dozen, and one of the thicker volumes was *Collier's Cyclopedia of Commercial and Social Information*. Published in 1892, the preface begins, "At no period in the history of the United States has the necessity for a cheap but perfect Cyclopedia of Useful Knowledge been so imperative. So keen is the competitive spirit of the age, that the advantage of knowledge in the struggle for advancement is apparent to all." This book goes beyond standard self-help as its chapters include Riding, Driving, Swimming, Drowning, Forms of Legal Documents, A Full Rigged Ship, Games of Cards, the Cultivation of Fruit, Poultry, and a Brief History of the United States to name a few. Naturally, there's a section on the Letter Writer and it provides these samples for how to best write or request a recommendation.

Introducing a Young Lady Seeking Employment

POUGHKEEPSIE, JUNE 1, 1882

Dear Mr. Jones:——

The young lady whom this letter will make known to you is desirous of obtaining employment in your city, and I use our old acquaintanceship as the bridge to your good offices in her behalf. She has received a very liberal education and would prove of immense value to a family whose young children need careful and judicious teaching. She is gentle, amiable, and willing. I trust you will be able to serve her.

I am, etc.,

Dear Mr. Jones, Your sincere friend, R.A. Appleton

Introducing a Gentleman Seeking a Position in a Counting-house

ALBANY, JUNE 1, 1882

My Dear Sir:

Recognizing your well-merited and extensive influence in the commercial circles in your city, I beg to introduce to you W. James Farms, who is desirous of obtaining a clerkship in a counting-house. He is a gentleman of capacity and ability. His character stands A 1, and he is as industrious as he is energetic. He considers New York a better field than this place, and prefers to try his chance there to remaining here. He can refer to me. Trusting that you will lend him a helping hand, I am,

Yours, very truly, *Jacob Hill*

From a Young Man to a Friend Soliciting a Situation

MOHAWK , MARCH 28, 1882

Dear Edward,

When you left Galveston, you were kind enough to promise that should it be in your power to forward my interest in any manner you would feel pleasure in so doing. I am now in want of a position, my former employer having sold his business, and his successor having, as he informs me, a sufficient number of hands for all the work he is likely to have. If, therefore, you should hear of any situation or employment which you consider likely to suit me, either in my own business, that of a clerk, or in any other in which I can make myself useful, your recommendation would greatly oblige, and be of material service to,

Dear Edward, Very Truly Yours, *John James*

Asking Permission to Refer a Person

NEW HAVEN, CONN. JULY 7, '82

Dear Sir:

As I have had the honor of being known to you for some years during which period I trust my conduct has impressed you favorably, I take the liberty of soliciting at your hand the following favor: Messrs. Sebthorp, of Beaver Street, New York, are in want of a correspondent at London, and as I am about to proceed there on some affairs of my own, and shall probably take my residence in that capital for some years, I am anxious to secure a post which appears to me in every way eligible, and accords with my views exactly.

As a matter of course, Messers. Sebthorp desire testimonials as to my capacity and integrity, and as you are in a position to speak positively on these points, I have written to ask you whether I may so far trespass on your kindness as to mention your name by way of reference.

Should you kindly grant this request, I need scarcely assure you that my endeavor will be to prove both to Messers. Sebthorp and yourself that you have not been mistaken in your opinion of me, while I shall ever feel grateful for this further instance of the interest evinced by you in the welfare of

Your truly obliged, Walter Mott

P.S. Final Thoughts

In the last days of writing this, my friend Bradley asked me what I planned to say about fountain pens. I looked at him blankly as I hadn't though specifically about fountain pens or any writing utensil for that matter. I felt overwhelmed, as I knew I would fall short of incorporating everything people think of when they think of writing letters. I told him I would try to squeeze something in but have been unable to thus far. So I leave you with his wise words, "Fountain pens are more romantic than ballpoint pens in the same way that LP records are more romantic than CDs, and wood fireplaces over those weird gas ones."

History and Its Volumes of Letters

Speaking of not being able to include everything I wanted to: One of my favorite parts of putting this book together has been compiling the historical letters. They are fascinating, voyeuristic windows into the past. This task was also overwhelming and frustrating, as I was bound to fall short of conveying the experience of being between the shelves and countless volumes of collected letters. Please know that I've hardly nicked the surface. I hardly scratched it. I've hardly even touched it. There are innumerable collections of letters written by notorious writers, politicians, philosophers, artists, and monarchs. If there's a figure you idolize who rose to the top in the mid 20th century or before, then there's a good chance that a volume of their letters is on a library shelf or rare bookstore near you.

Collected letters offer a glimpse into someone's life more intimate than any biography. And they're still coming. In the spring of 2006 an exhibition of never-before-seen letters, postcards, and other notes from Anne Frank and her family opened at the Amsterdam Historical Museum. In summer of 2006 the last of Albert Einstein's personal family letters were displayed for the public to see—revealing the details of a very difficult time in his life—and plans for publication are in the works. And surely someday they'll publish a great volume of your letters—provided you write some.

The Key to Letter Writing

If you've stuck with me this long, then I owe you the secret to the sauce. The essential ingredient in a letter that will surely make its mark on someone's memory is not necessarily in the wording but in the fact that you noticed. Letters are a way of letting someone know you caught them. You caught them being kind. You caught them being clever. You caught them being sexy. You caught them doing the right thing when everyone else told them it was wrong. You noticed them when they thought no one was looking, and then you fixed it on the page and gave it permanence.

This rings true even with letters that have angry or frustrated content, because you're noticing that someone stopped noticing you, or that they don't notice their actions hurt you and as a result your relationship is suffering. With sympathy letters you're noticing the life of the deceased and the grief of the person in mourning. In apology letters you're noticing that you did someone wrong and are coming clean about it. With politically charged letters you notice that there is severe injustice going on. To write effective letters, pay close attention. This, if nothing else, is the one thing we're all doing here, trying to get ourselves noticed—even if it's just by one other person. And this is why writing a letter can make you part of someone's life forever.

Well, this is my stop. I get off here and leave you to write the letters of your life. Good luck and enjoy. Thank you for taking this journey with me.

With grateful and endless enthusiasm, $Samara$

ACKNOWLEDGMENTS

The Creator: Author of life and lover of concord, thank you for the sun, the wind, and the rain. Thank you for smiles and surprises. Thank you for disguising life's greatest opportunities as seemingly insurmountable challenges. And thank you, thank you, thank you (I will never be able to thank you enough) for putting the following people in my path:

The Editor: The lovely Miss Anne Cole, you made this project not only painless but quite pleasant I'd say. Thank you for your enthusiasm, guidance, grace, shrewd insights and jovial girl talk. I started with an editor and ended with a friend.

The Mentor: The counselor, the financial advisor, the psychotherapist, and (oh yeah) my agent. Adam Chromy, you are the most honest man I have ever met. Can I take you shopping with me? Thank you for knowing something about everything and for letting me in on the important parts. This would not have turned out so well without your direction. I will reach my full potential working with you—this much I know is true.

The On-Call Editor: Elise, first of all I love that you reminded me to put you on the acknowledgments page. You know, because I was gonna forget. Goofy girl! Thank you for reading basically everything I've ever written from the pitches to the proposals and all the e-mails to (and from) the boys. How do I love thee? Let me count the ways!

The On-Call Copy Editors: Alexa, Rachel, and Sarah, thank you for dotting all my i's and crossing all my t's (and making sure those apostrophes are correct) on more than one occasion. Thank you also for being the on-call friends and generous advice givers.

The Surrogate Mother: Zazel, what I wouldn't give to go back and live in the 1960s in New York City with you. Oh well, I'm glad to have you now. Thank you for your constant care that didn't stop when the job did. In my perfect world, we eat lunch together every day.

The Friends: Who unceasingly support me and my absurd ideas. Tom, thanks for your readymade support and coming up with a financial plan for my Web site. I'll put it into practice someday, I promise. Miss Jenée, thank you for being my reliable dinner date and travel partner and also for announcing my forthcoming book to all strangers present. Erica, thanks for having the most amusing dating life of anyone I've ever met, and thank you especially for asking me to write a letter to what's-his-face. Lori, thank you for all the thank-you notes and for sticking around for ten years. Bradley, thank you for swooping in at the eleventh hour and voluntarily listening to me go on and on (and on) about this project—and for adding your alternative wisdom. Neal, thank you for going to see the Al Gore movie with me at 9 o'clock on a Monday. Allison, fellow author and dynamite editor, thank you for your advice and support—not to mention fabulous collection of Victorian etiquette books.

The DailyCandy Diva: Jeralyn, as promised, you get my firstborn. Thank you for responding so readily to a virtual stranger and for featuring my Web site. I hope you're admiring your handiwork, my friend.

The Ex-Boyfriend: Jesse, if all exes were as close as we are, the world would be a better place. If I ever accomplish anything it'll be from trying to keep up with you. Thank you for your unyielding friendship and all the wonderful letters you've written me.

The Family: The Stroup Von Trapp family that is. If I could give the world a gift, I would multiply you all by the millions (imagine that!). You are an indestructible support system that every person should have access to. Thank you for being the caring, reliable, rowdy, hilarious, and intrepid village that raised me. As for the O'Shea side of the family: Gerry, I attribute all pop-culture references in this book to you. Thanks for my early education.

The Sister: Andrea Lynn O'Shea—the same mysterious "Lynn" who wrote the beautiful letter in Chapter 1 (it's a long story). Dare I attempt to return such a perfect sentiment to the little sister who somehow grew past me in practical wisdom? What a gift you are—how wonderful to have someone who requires that I say nothing and still understands everything. Now, will you stop counting and write your first book already?

The Parents: Heroes are tall and small. Some have lots of facial hair while others have none. Thank you both for being my forever frame of reference for how to: work hard, lend support, handle rainy days, and make the most of marriage. Believe it or not, I've been paying attention.

Those Who Have Gone Before: David Jerome Stroup (grandfather): As if my obsession with language and memorizing random pieces of poetry could come from anywhere else. How I wish you were here to share this with me. I miss you so much. Barbara O'Shea (grandma): The quiet caregiver, thank you for being so selfless and giving your family so much. Irene (aunt): Thank you for telling me the story of the stars. Megan Louise (dear friend): I have an idea. Let's meet back at Lake Champion. You stay in the kitchen with Cookie and make fun of me for flirting shamelessly with Scott (guilty). We'll complain about being tired and stay up all night anyway. Thank you for always making me smile—then and now.

Sources and Permissions

All letters and electronic mail written to the author appear with full permission of the charming, attractive, and astute people who wrote them. Yes, even the heartbreakers.

Introduction Part Two: Letter Writing and the Internet

Student Newspaper Quote:
The Duquesne Duke, "If Love Fails Buy a Letter," by Chris Young. October 13, 2005. Volume 85, Number 9, Page 3.

Love Letters

Signing Off:
Davidson, Cathy N. *The Book of Love.* New York: Penguin Group, 1992.
Lowenherz, David H. *The 50 Greatest Love Letters of All Time.* Crown Publishers: New York, 2002.
Keats Letter:
Originally published in 1878 in *Letters of John Keats to Fanny Brawne* (Scribner, Armstrong & Co.) Available online at englishhistory.net.

Erotic Letters

Anaïs Nin Quote:
Nin, Anaïs. *Little Birds.* From the short story *A Model.* Orlando: Harcourt, 1979.
Song of Solomon Verse:
The Bible with the Apocrypha: New Revised Standard Version. London: Collins Publishers, 1989.

James Joyce Excerpt:
Ellmann, Richard. *The Selected Letters of James Joyce.* New York: The Viking Press, 1966, 1975.

Good-bye Letters

Signing Off:
Davidson, Cathy N. *The Book of Love.* New York: Penguin Group, 1992.
Holmes, Anna. *Hell Hath No Fury: Women's Letters from the End of the Affair.* New York: Ballantine Books, 2002.
McLynn, Frank. *Famous Letters: Messages and Thoughts that Shaped Our World.* A Reader's Digest Book. Pleasantville, New York, 1993.
Antoinette Letter:
Mayer, Dorothy Moulton. *Marie Antoinette: The Tragic Queen.* New York: Coward-McCann, Inc, 1968.

Flaming-tongue Letters

Signing Off:
Associated Press Article: *Letters Show Different Side of Anne Frank: Museum Displays Correspondence Never Before Open to the Public,* by Arthur Max. April 11, 2006.
Poe Letter:
Poe-Allan-Ellis Papers, 1803–1881, MS. C 38, Valentine Richmond History Center, Richmond, Virginia. Available online at the Edgar Allan Poe Society of Baltimore Web site: eapoe.org.

Breakup Letters

Signing Off:
Holmes, Anna. *Hell Hath No Fury: Women's Letters from the End of the Affair.* New York: Ballantine Books, 2002.

Bernhardt Letter:
Gold, Arthur, and Robert Fizdale. *The Divine Sarah: A Life of Sarah Bernhardt*. New York: Knopf, 1991.

Unauthorized Love Letters

Foster to Griswold Quote:
Silverman, Kenneth. *Edgar A. Poe: Mournful and Never-ending Remembrance*. New York: HarperCollins, 1991.
Beethoven Letter:
Originally published in 1840. Available online at all-about-beethoven.com.

Thank-you Letters

Signing Off:
Brown, Helen Gurley. *Dear Pussycat: Mash Notes and Missives from the Desk of Cosmopolitan's Legendary Editor*. New York: St. Martin's Press, 2004.
Gold, Arthur, and Robert Fizdale. *The Divine Sarah: A Life of Sarah Bernhardt*. New York: Knopf, 1991.
Post, Emily. *Etiquette in Society, in Business, Politics, and at Home*. Funk and Wagnalls, 1922. Available online at Gutenberg.org.

Apology Letters

Mansfield Letter and Explanation of Nickname Tig:
Murry, John Middleton. *Katherine Mansfield's Letters to John Middleton Murry*. New York: Alfred A. Knopf, 1951. Letter reprinted with permission of the Society of Authors as the literary representative of the Estate of Katherine Mansfield.

Sympathy Letters

Brown, Helen Gurley. *Dear Pussycat: Mash Notes and Missives from the Desk of Cosmopolitan's Legendary Editor.* New York: St. Martin's Press, 2004.

Post Excerpt:
Post, Emily. *Etiquette in Society, in Business, Politics, and at Home.* Funk and Wagnalls, 1922. Available online at Gutenberg.org.
Lincoln Letter:
Originally published in *The Boston Transcript,* November 25, 1864. Available online at the Abraham Lincoln Association Web site: Alincolnassoc.com.

Letters Requesting Acts of Amnesty

Amnesty International Letter Writing Guide:
Reprinted with permission of Amnesty International USA (amnestyusa.org).
Stanton to Anthony Letter:
Stanton, Theodore and Blanch, Harriot Stanton ed. *Elizabeth Cady Stanton as Revealed in Her Letters, Diary, and Reminiscences.* New York: Harper & Brothers, 1922.
Anthony to Stanton Letter:
Elizabeth Cady Stanton Papers, Box 1, Folder: General Correspondence 1856–59. Manuscript Division, Library of Congress, Washington D.C.
Anthony Court Case Quote and the Letter that Changed It All:
One Woman, One Vote. An Educational Film Center Production, 1995. Distributed by PBS video.

Letters to the Editor

Vogue Letters:
"Talking Back: Letters from Readers" *Vogue*, November, 2005.
"Letters from France and England" *Vogue*, July 15, 1940.

Business Letters

Signing Off:
McLynn, Frank. *Famous Letters: Messages and Thoughts that Shaped Our World*. A Reader's Digest Book. Pleasantville, New York, 1993.
Carnegie Letter:
Reprinted with permission of the Carnegie Corporation of New York (carnegie.org).

Recommendation Letters

Collier's Cyclopedia Letters:
Collier's Cyclopedia of Commercial and Social Information. New York: P. F. Collier, 1892.